WW2 in Europe

Great Battles for Boys

Joe Giorello

with
Sibella Giorello

Great Battles for Boys: WWII Europe

Dedicated to my sons Daniel and Nico.
And every soldier missing in action.

CONTENTS

NOTE FROM THE AUTHOR

In the battle for freedom, great men make great sacrifices. Why? Because freedom isn't free. Usually it comes at a high price. As you'll see from the battles in this book, men pay for freedom with their lives.

This book will show you what happened in some of the world's greatest battles. You'll also see what warriors can teach us about courage and determination and fighting, especially when the odds are stacked against them.

I hope you'll also follow the links at the end of each chapter and discover even more good books, Internet sites, and movies you can watch with your whole family—but remember most of those movies were made in Hollywood, so they're not the literal truth. After reading this book, you'll probably see the difference between truth and fiction.

I enjoy hearing from my readers. If you have questions or want to suggest another battle for a future book, contact me on the Great Battles page at Facebook at facebook.com/greatbattles. And be sure to check out the other books in the Great Battles series. Enjoy your journey into great battles, and remember, "Freedom isn't free."

—Joe Giorello

PRELUDE TO WAR

Adolf Hitler, 1937

"WARS AND RUMORS of wars." People have been saying that phrase for thousands of years. You've probably heard it yourself.

But why has that one phrase lasted so long? Because wars don't just fall from the sky. Conflicts erupt from a sequence of events. Long before war begins, people are talking about those big events—"rumors of war."

For World War II, the sequence of events leading up to it actually began with World War I. That war was called "The Great War," not because it was so good, but because so many men lost their lives—about twenty million casualties in Germany, Russia, France, and England. More than 300,000 Americans also died in the war.

That's a lot of people.

However, when WWI ended in 1918, the circumstances that started the war hadn't been fully resolved. Some of these circumstances are complicated, but everyone can agree on these facts: Germany started WWI, the war almost wrecked Europe, and four years later, Germany lost. Because the war inflicted so much pain and suffering, France wanted to punish Germany, even after the Germans had surrendered.

Therefore, France added some harsh rules to the peace agreement, called the Treaty of Versailles.

For instance, the Treaty of Versailles ordered Germany to pay a huge amount of money to the winning countries, such as France. That's not unusual. Winners sometimes demand a losing country pay back the debts created by a war—a process called "reparations." However, Germany was completely broke after WWI. Its people were literally starving and couldn't find jobs.

England and America asked France to lighten up. For one

thing, how was Germany going to pay money to other countries when it couldn't take care of itself? England and the United States were also worried that the treaty's terms might actually make things worse. The German people would resent the treaty, leading to bitterness that could start another war.

But France wouldn't listen.

So, the Treaty of Versailles was ratified, or made official.

Germany was forced to obey all the treaty's demands.

Unfortunately, just as England and America predicted, things only got worse. The struggling German people grew even angrier at France and the other countries that won WWI.

As that anger and resentment spread among the Germans, a powerful madman arose to take charge. This man would change the world—for the worse.

His name was Adolf Hitler.

Massive German crowds gather to cheer Hitler, standing in the window, after being inaugurated as Germany's chancellor on January 30, 1933

During WWI, Hitler served in the German Army and was awarded several medals for bravery. After the Great War, he rose through the German government, gathering political steam with former soldiers like himself who really hated the Treaty of Versailles. But not everyone liked Hitler. Some German politicians threw him in jail. But while he was in prison, Hitler grew even more popular by writing his autobiography, *Mein Kampf* (pronounced *"mine komph"*), which means "my struggle."

In this book, Hitler told the German people they were superior, that they belonged to something called the Aryan race. Hitler said these Aryans—people with blue eyes and light skin and blond hair—were greater than any other people on earth. And because they were better, Germany had a "historic destiny" to rule the world. The problem, Hitler said, was that some other people, especially Jews, were holding Germany back from true greatness. If Germany got rid of all the non-Aryan people, Germany could become powerful again. No more hunger. No more looking for jobs. No more trouble.

Hitler's message filled a lot of German people with hope. They believed his ideas would change their lives for the better.

Children were taught at a young age to worship Hitler. Here, schoolchildren give the Nazi salute. 1934

When Hitler got out of jail, he was even more popular. He was also learning to speak with passion and persuasion by watching the political speeches of Benito Mussolini, the dictator of Italy. As head of Italy's Fascist party, Mussolini drew huge crowds wherever he went. Hitler and Mussolini agreed about many things—such as the government should be extremely powerful and rule over people's lives. Soon these two men formed a political alliance.

Meanwhile, Hitler and his party of Nazis—or National Socialists—were winning more political offices. Hitler was creating military-type organizations within the government by backing people who agreed with his idea that Germany should rule the world and that the country needed to "cleanse" itself of all non-Aryan races—especially Jewish people. Eventually, Hitler won control of the entire German government, giving the Nazis full power over the country.

Hitler continued to give speeches about this new Germany, an empire that would "last for a thousand years." He called that empire the Third Reich.

To build that empire, Hitler wanted to take back the land that the Treaty of Versailles forced Germany to give up—land given to other countries, such as Poland. And Poland turned out to be Hitler's first military target.

His sneaky attack on that country would kill thousands— and launch what would become World War II.

THE INVASION OF POLAND

September 1, 1939

German soldiers march into Poland, 1939

HAVE YOU EVER watched a little kid play with their favorite toy? If you suddenly take away the toy, the kid will naturally get upset. But what if you give the toy to another kid—somebody the kid doesn't even like? The kid will be even more upset!

You've created a major problem.

The German people typically didn't like the Polish people. So when the Treaty of Versailles forced Germany to give land to Poland, it was like a kid seeing a cherished toy handed over to their enemy. With every passing year, Germans grew more upset about that land switch.

Look at the map. It shows Germany in 1939, marked in black. To the immediate right is the land given to Poland, marked in dark gray, with Poland itself to the left of that in lighter gray.

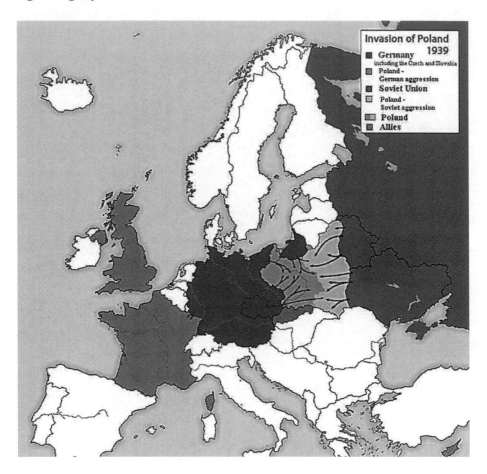

With the German people upset about their bad economy and this land switch, Hitler cleverly played on their emotions. He kept saying that the land belonged to Germany, not Poland.

At the same time, Hitler was fooling the rest of the world. Right after saying these things to his own people, he turned around and signed a "nonaggression" pact with Poland. This pact meant Hitler was promising not to attack Poland.

This confused the German people. How could Germany regain that land if Hitler wasn't going to invade Poland?

Here's how—Hitler was patient and evil. After signing that pact, Hitler and some other German politicians got together and made up some lies about Poland. They accused the Poles of all kinds of terrible things, and German newspapers reported these accusations as if they were facts. This is called propaganda—when the truth gets twisted to support a political agenda.

Hitler also started accusing the Polish government of killing innocent Germans who lived on the land that was taken away by the Versailles Treaty. Naturally, the German people were outraged by this "news."

But Hitler's propaganda didn't end there. In late August 1939, some German spies seized a Polish radio station. The spies dressed up like native Poles and started broadcasting an ugly report about Germans—all spoken in Polish, of course. To make their lies seem even more believable, the spies dragged some dead bodies to the radio station to "prove" the Poles had killed some Germans. The same night, these spies created even more "crimes" against Germans who were living in Poland, including setting a house on fire.

Of course, the German people demanded justice. All these lies were part of Hitler's plan to invade Poland, a plan that was named "Operation Himmler." Yes, Hitler had signed the nonaggression pact with Poland, but he was devising ways to break the agreement. Hitler didn't care if everything was based on lies.

"The victor will not be asked whether he told the truth," Hitler said.

Right after those radio station "murders," Germany's air

force—called the Luftwaffe—started bombing Polish cities, bridges, roads, airfields, and communication centers.

Thousands of innocent people were killed.

After the Luftwaffe struck, hordes of German tanks roared into the country, smashing through villages, towns, and markets.

Then the German infantry marched in, shooting to kill.

The date was September 1, 1939. It would mark the beginning of World War II.

Two days later, on September 3, Great Britain, France, Australia, and New Zealand declared war on Germany.

But for the Polish people, help was too late.

Invading German vehicles shove aside a horse-drawn Polish cart

Poland never really trusted Hitler, even after he had signed the nonaggression pact. Most Polish leaders suspected Hitler would try something sneaky.

However, nobody expected a sudden ruthless attack on civilians.

Germany was demonstrating its new style of warfare called Blitzkrieg or "lightning war." This tactic worked like a sucker punch—coming out of nowhere so fast that the victim doesn't have time to recover and respond.

The Luftwaffe smothered the Polish sky with bombers and fighter planes while massive concentrations of armored and motorized infantry stormed across the land, shattering any enemy defenses. Blitzkrieg not only surprised the enemy, it created so much chaos that opposing military leaders struggled to organize their defenses.

In the case of this invasion, the situation was even worse for the Polish military because its soldiers were still using outdated weapons and tactics that were used during WWI. Cavalry soldiers spurred horses toward armored German tanks and swung swords against machine gun fire. Wooden and canvas biplanes were shot out of the sky by modern German fighter planes, such as the Messerschmitt 109.

Polish cavalry soldier, 1938

Yet, despite being the total underdog, Polish soldiers fought bravely.

Three squadrons of Polish cavalry soldiers attacked the German 8th Army and forced them to retreat. Under heavy machine gun fire, the horseback-riding soldiers pursued the Germans and managed to capture one of the Germans' division headquarters, taking captive one general and about a hundred soldiers.

Unfortunately, the Blitzkrieg tactic confused the Polish army's high command. It sent troops to the wrong defensive positions, allowing German ground forces to break right through the lines.

Lone horse, stranded in a Polish battlefield, September 1939

As if this wasn't enough trouble, on September 17, troops from the Soviet Union invaded Poland's eastern border. (Look at that map, above. To the right, you'll see where Stalin's forces invaded). It turned out Hitler had another secret—he and Soviet leader Josef Stalin had agreed to take over Poland and divide the country between themselves.

This second invasion prompted Poland's commander in chief and several other officials to flee into Romania.

However, the attack still wasn't over.

The Luftwaffe unleashed the first large-scale aerial bombardment on a major city, hitting Bzura, Poland. For ten days, the outmanned Polish forces tried to fight the advancing German 8th Army. But every counterattack failed. The Luftwaffe destroyed all the bridges across the Bzura River, trapping the Polish forces in an open area where German Stuka bombers pounded them even further.

When the anti-aircraft ammunition ran out, Polish forces

retreated into nearby forests, but the Germans kept pursuing them. German planes dropped incendiaries—burning weapons—that flushed the men from the trees.

During this one campaign, the Germans dropped hundreds—perhaps thousands—of bombs.

Young survivor of the Luftwaffe bombing of Warsaw, Poland, 1939

Polish cities burned to the ground.

The Luftwaffe targeted civilians, even refugees who were fleeing the cities. Mass killing was all part of Blitzkrieg's tactics to completely destroy an enemy and create panic. Far away from the battles, German secret police were murdering thousands of Polish people.

During this September campaign, the German military killed between 150,000–200,000 civilians.

Finally, on September 27, 1939, Poland surrendered to Germany.

More than 300,000 Polish soldiers were captured as prisoners of war. Hitler and Stalin divided the country, just as they planned, and then both dictators turned their sights on the rest of Europe.

Hitler and Stalin both wanted more land. And they would kill to get it.

This was war.

WHO FOUGHT?

The secret plan to launch WWII was code named Operation Himmler. Who was Himmler?

Heinrich Himmler was one of Hitler's leading henchmen. He joined the Nazi party in 1923 and helped Hitler rise to power.

Himmler coordinated Nazi propaganda. When Hitler needed an excuse to invade Poland, Himmler came up with those false stories for the newspapers. He also coordinated the fake murders at the Polish radio station. Himmler hated Jews and became one of the chief strategists for the mass murder of millions of innocent people who Hitler considered "inferior" races. That mass murder was later called the Holocaust. You'll read about it in later chapters.

When Himmler was growing up, his family was part of the Catholic church. But Himmler left the church as he grew closer to Hitler. He became obsessed with the occult—the dark magic of superstition. Himmler designed many of the symbols that the Nazis used to identify themselves.

For instance, Hitler had handpicked some fanatic followers to form an elite group called the SS. These soldiers were ruthless beyond imagination, and Himmler gave the SS its public symbol—two lightning bolts, side by side. The symbol was based on ancient German mythology. The SS wore this symbol on their uniforms. Before long, the symbol struck fear in people because it represented merciless pain and oppression.

FIND OUT MORE:

BOOKS

Blitzkrieg: The German Invasion of Poland and France 1939 to 1940 by Phil Yates

Hitler Youth: Growing Up in Hitler's Shadow by Susan Campbell Bartoletti

World War II: An Interactive History Adventure by Elizabeth Raum

DK Eyewitness Books: World War II by Simon Adams

INTERNET

Read the diary of a Polish doctor who witnessed the Nazi takeover of his country: www.eyewitnesstohistory.com/poland.htm

This short documentary on YouTube shows historical footage of the invasion: youtube.com/watch?v=uNOqSSP1o94

Watch the Blitzkrieg in action: youtube.com/watch?v=vgCWMZaKKUw

MOVIES

The Waffen SS: Hitler's Elite Fighting Force

THE WINTER WAR

November 30, 1939 to March 13, 1940

Finnish soldiers in a snow-walled machine gun battery during the Winter War

HITLER AND STALIN agreed to divide Poland between themselves. They also promised not to attack each other.

After Germany invaded Poland, Hitler pushed his forces west toward France and England, while Stalin clamped his iron fist around the territories closer to Russia's borders—Estonia, Latvia, and Lithuania. These countries quickly fell to the Russian Soviet Communists.

But one country that shared a border with Russia held onto its independence—Finland.

Finland sits at the far northern tip of Europe (see map below). What Stalin wanted was a narrow strip of land inside Finland that connected Russia to southern Finland. It was called the Karelian Isthmus, and it was ideal for naval and air bases.

At first, Finnish diplomats tried to negotiate with Stalin and talk him out of being so aggressive.

However, on November 30, 1939, Stalin sent about 120,000 troops to the isthmus with 1,500 armored vehicles.

Map of northern Europe, before 1939. See the narrow isthmus (center right) linking southern Finland with the Soviet Union.

The Finns were horribly outnumbered. They only had 21,000 soldiers and some anti-tank guns.

This David-versus-Goliath battle was called the Winter War.

Finland asked other countries for help fighting Stalin's forces, but only its neighbor Sweden responded. At the outbreak of WWII, Sweden had declared itself neutral, but it supplied Finland with ammunition, small arms, some airplanes, and artillery.

Those supplies didn't look like enough to beat Stalin. But the Finnish troops proved to be physically strong, well-disciplined, and excellent marksmen. They also took on the Soviet threat with a fighting spirit. When one Finnish soldier heard about the massive Soviet army coming across the border, he said, "There are so many Russians, and our country so small, where will we find room to bury them all?"

The Finns spread their troops across the country. Some were stationed on the eastern border to intercept Soviet invaders. Since the heaviest fighting would be on the isthmus, Finnish troops amassed along the Mannerheim Line, named for their leader, Marshal Carl Gustaf Mannerheim.

While the Soviets outnumbered the Finns almost five to one, they had some serious problems. First of all, Stalin was jealous of anybody who might be more intelligent or powerful than himself. To make sure no one would challenge him, Stalin executed his best military leaders or banished them to labor camps. As a result, his army was often disorganized and poorly trained.

The Soviets also struggled against Finland's terrain and weather.

The bitter cold made everything more difficult, including

flying. Soviet pilots rarely got off the ground because at Finland's far latitude, there were few daylight hours. Another problem was the Soviets' dark uniforms. Marching across the snow-white landscape, the Soviet soldiers were clear targets for the Finns.

Regardless of how many Soviet soldiers were killed, Stalin just sent more.

During the Winter War, reindeer carried supplies and towed sleds into battles

Vastly outnumbered, the Finns needed better tactics to beat their enemy. For instance, Finnish infantry units wore white camouflage and skied across the terrain, encircling and isolating the Soviet troops. Other times, they snuck up silently and took out men using their knives. Since both sides were using similar weapons, they stole the Soviet guns and ammunition. Working in four-man teams, they also dropped logs across the snowy paths used by the Soviet tanks. The tank soldiers were forced to stop their vehicle to remove the obstructions, and then the Finns would hurl poor-man grenades at them. These grenades were just glass bottles filled with flammable liquids, usually gasoline or alcohol, with a cotton wick stuck in the bottle's mouth for a fuse.

The Finns called these homemade grenades Molotov cocktails, named after the Soviet's foreign minister.

In all, the tiny Finnish force managed to destroy about 2,000 Soviet tanks.

As the battle continued into January, temperatures dropped even further. It was one of the coldest winters on record.

However, the Finns kept up the fight.

During one confrontation, Finland's 9th Division fractured a Soviet column into smaller units, killing more than 17,000 enemy troops. The Finns lost only 250 men in that action.

One Finnish soldier's Molotov cocktail for the Winter War

At Lake Tolvajarvi, fewer than one hundred Finns destroyed an entire Soviet battalion of about 800 men—within minutes. The Finns suffered only one casualty, a soldier who had a heart attack but survived.

Soon the Soviets realized this little enemy was much tougher than expected.

The Soviets were especially afraid of the Finnish snipers. Men like Simo Hayha. A farmer by trade, Hayha joined Finland's 34th Infantry Regiment during the Winter War and used a simple iron-sighted rifle.

Within three months, Hayha had killed more than 500 Russians—a record that remains unmatched to this day.

In all—between the skiing infantry, the Molotov cocktails, and the snipers—the Finns killed, wounded, or captured about 500,000 Soviet troops.

Finally, Stalin realized he couldn't win this battle.

On March 12, 1940, Finland and the Soviet Union signed the Moscow Peace Treaty.

In exchange for peace, Finland agreed to give the Soviets about ten percent of its territory and thirty percent of its economic assets.

One Soviet military leader grumbled, "We gained 22,000 square miles of territory. Just enough to bury our dead."

Finland paid a price for keeping its independence—more than 25,000 casualties.

Also, remember the promise that Hitler and Stalin made to not attack each other? It didn't last. Hitler and Stalin were soon fighting each other, and about a year after the Winter War, the Soviets once again tried to invade Finland.

This time, the Finns decided to get more help. They didn't like the Nazis, but they wanted to keep their independence. So they went with that old adage that says "The enemy of my enemy is my friend."

To hold back Stalin, Finland aligned itself with Germany and kept its independence.

In fact, during WWII, Finland was the only European country outside Great Britain that was never occupied by enemy forces.

Once again, David beat Goliath.

WHO FOUGHT?

Lauri Allan Törni is the only soldier known to fight for three different countries: Finland, Germany, and the United States.

During the Winter War, he was a Finnish captain and led an infantry company, distinguishing himself for annihilating Russian divisions. When Finland later aligned itself with Germany, Törni was sent to Austria for officer training and became part of Hitler's forces.

After WWII, Törni worked on a Swedish cargo ship. He jumped overboard in the Gulf of Mexico, swimming to Mobile, Alabama. He then became a political refugee in the United States. In 1953, Congress granted him residency, and the next year he joined the US Army.

In America, he adopted the name Larry Thorne and earned a place within the military Special Forces. Thorne taught everything from skiing and survival strategies to guerrilla tactics. He rose through the ranks, earning two Purple Hearts and one Bronze Star. During his second tour in Vietnam in 1965, he transferred from the 5th Special Forces Group to a classified special operations unit focused on unconventional warfare.

On October 18, 1965, Thorne was supervising a secret mission when his helicopter crashed into a mountainous area.

Rescue teams were unable to locate the crash site.

In 1999, Thorne's remains were recovered and brought back to the United States.

Today, United States Major Larry Thorne—a.k.a. Finnish Captain and German officer Lauri Allan Törni—is buried at Arlington National Cemetery near other bodies recovered from that secret Vietnam mission.

BOOKS

The Winter War: The Soviet Attack on Finland, 1939–1940 by Eloise
     Engle and Lauri Paananen

World War II Winter and Mountain Warfare Tactics by Stephen Bull

INTERNET

Fire and Ice is an independent film about the Winter War. It combines historical footage with reenactments. Available through PBS, the film has been partially uploaded to YouTube:
youtube.com/watch?v=WR2FqMUVZzc

Fire and Ice also developed a website about the Winter War:
media.wfyi.org/fireandice

Be sure to check out the website's *Weapons* link which explains the Molotov cocktail:
media.wfyi.org/fireandice/history/molotov_cocktail.htm

THE BATTLESHIP BISMARCK

Photo # NH 59672   German battleship Bismarck, stern view

REMEMBER HOW THE Treaty of Versailles demanded Germany pay money to the countries involved in World War I?

The treaty also said Germany couldn't build a large army for itself. Germany was allowed only 100,000 soldiers. No tanks. No air force. No submarines. Only six large warships.

Just as Hitler found ways to get around the nonaggression

pact with Poland, he grew Germany's military beyond the treaty's limits. As early as 1933, he was already rearming troops. Six years later, he and his generals had developed the world's most powerful air force, army, and navy which allowed them to inflict Blitzkrieg warfare.

After invading Poland, Germany defeated Norway, Holland, and Belgium—within months.

France also looked close to being conquered.

By 1940, England was the only large European country that stood firmly opposed to Hitler's plans. The legendary British navy had ruled the seas for several centuries. Meanwhile, the German navy, or *Kriegsmarine*, relied on its U-boats—submarines that traveled in wolf packs.

Hitler decided the best way to crush England and ruin its morale was by beating its navy into submission.

So he built the *Bismarck*.

Launched in 1939, the *Bismarck* was a stunning battleship. From its bow (front end) to its stern (back end), the Bismarck stretched 823 feet. From port (left side) to starboard (right), it spread 118 feet. Despite weighing about 50,000 tons, the *Bismarck* could reach speeds of 30 knots (about 34 mph) because it was powered by three steam engines and twelve superheated boilers. The *Bismarck* also had two rudders.

Remember those two rudders. They will become very important later.

The ship was protected by 13-inch-thick armor plates, eight 15-inch guns, and twelve 6-inch guns. It also carried four floatplanes, 108 officers, and 1,962 enlisted men, all under the command of Admiral Gunther Lutjens and Captain Ernst Lindermann.

In the spring of 1940, the Germans planned to sneak the

Bismarck into the North Atlantic Ocean and sink every single merchant ship belonging to the Allies.

The Allies were all the countries that had united against Germany and Italy (and later Japan). Meanwhile, the opposing countries that banded together with Hitler were called the Axis.

When all the Allied ships were destroyed, Hitler planned to invade England.

The entire plan relied on the mighty *Bismarck*.

THE BREAKOUT

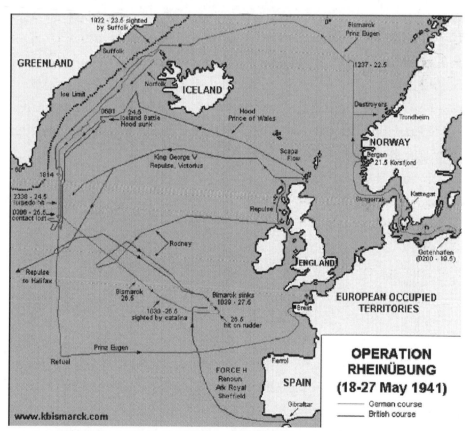

Arrows indicate the path of German and British navies. Map courtesy of kbismarck.com.

On May 20, 1940, under cover of rain and fog, the *Bismarck* and another German ship, the *Prinz Eugen*, slipped undetected past the coast of Norway and crossed into the North Sea.

In the early morning hours of May 21, the British cruiser *Suffolk* spotted the *Bismarck* and radioed London. The *Suffolk* pursued the German ships into the fog. Another British ship, *Norfolk*, joined in the pursuit. (See map, above.)

Then British Home Fleet Commander Admiral Jack Tovey dispatched the battleship *Prince of Wales* with its 14-inch guns. Unfortunately, the pride of the British navy—the battleship *Hood*—was more than 300 miles away. Before the *Bismarck* was built, the *Hood* was the most powerful ship in the world. It weighed 48,000 tons, stretched 860 feet, and carried eight 15-inch guns.

The *Hood* sailed toward the pursuit. By May 24, the *Hood* and *Prince of Wales* were on an intercepting course, headed straight for the *Bismarck* and the *Prinz Eugen*.

When they were close to the Germans, the British battleships sounded alarms for battle stations. The *Hood* targeted *Prinz Eugen*.

Prince of Wales aimed her guns at the *Bismarck*.

But just as dawn was breaking, Admiral Lutjens suddenly changed course by shifting to port. This maneuver placed the *Bismarck* and *Prinz Eugen* in perfect positions to unleash all guns broadside on the *Hood* and *Prince of Wales*, both of which were still positioned with forward guns ready to fire.

The *Bismarck* opened fire with a roar like thunder. Her first salvo missed the *Hood*. The second scored a small hit. By the fifth salvo, the *Bismarck*'s gunners were finding their marks, landing at least one shell broadside into the *Hood*'s deck. That shell exploded in the magazine, where the ammunition is stored, setting off an even larger explosion.

As smoke billowed from the *Hood*, the next enormous explosion destroyed the ship. Within minutes, it was sinking.

Of the 1,500 men onboard the *Hood*, only three survived.

Battleship *Bismarck* withdrawing from the Battle of Denmark Strait after sinking *HMS Hood*, May 24, 1941. Photo courtesy of German archives.

German Captain Lindermann wanted to go after the *Prince of Wales*, but Admiral Lutjens said their original orders were to attack British convoys. As the two officers discussed their dilemma, they learned that the *Bismarck* had taken three hits, including one at port-bow that penetrated two oil tanks.

The ship was losing about 1,000 tons of fuel.

The German naval officers had another dilemma—should they continue their mission to destroy convoy ships or return to base for repairs?

Lutjens decided on the latter. He headed toward France.

Meanwhile, shocked by the loss of the mighty *Hood*, the British navy sent out wireless messages asking for all available ships to come and attack the *Bismarck*. Since the *Prince of Wales* and *Norfolk* were still following the Germans, Admiral Lutjens decided that *Prinz Eugen* should split off, take a separate route and possibly finish the mission to sink Allied convoys.

But Lutjens had another problem to deal with. The British aircraft carrier *Victorious* was hunting them down with enough power to launch Swordfish torpedo planes.

On the night of May 24, nine Swordfish attacked the *Bismarck*. Lutjens put the ship on a zigzag pattern, trying to escape the torpedoes. He also opened fire with everything on the ship, including her 15-inch guns. Because of the diversion tactics, the Swordfish planes didn't inflict much damage, and only one torpedo from the *Victorious* struck the *Bismarck*, doing little to stop the ship.

Shadowed by *Prince of Wales* and the *Norfolk*, Lutjens devised a brilliant plan. He told Captain Lindermann to sail the *Bismarck* west, then north. That path would place the ship *behind* her pursuers.

The plan worked to perfection.

By 3:30 a.m., the British lost track of both ships, and the fleet headed out in every direction to find them.

But German pride caused destruction.

Watching his brilliant plan at work, Lutjens sent out a thirty-minute message to the German naval headquarters in Paris, explaining what just happened. But every British radio detector in the North Atlantic heard his explanation.

The British were able to relocate the *Bismarck* within a fifty-mile radius. But they assumed the *Bismarck* was sailing back to Germany, so they dispatched ships in the wrong direction.

Captain Lindermann assured the *Bismarck*'s crew they would reach a French port by noon on May 26 and receive U-boat and Luftwaffe support. However, bad weather forced the *Bismarck* to remain at sea.

Floatplanes coming off the British ship *Ark Royal* spotted the *Bismarck*. When Admiral Tovey received the message, he suddenly realized his fleet heading for Germany had little chance of catching the ship. But Tovey was a committed fighter. He ordered all ships to head toward the *Bismarck*. In the meantime, he hoped the torpedo planes from the *Ark Royal* could slow down the Germans and allow the British fleet to catch up, even though the Swordfish planes were biplanes from the 1930s with a top speed of only 95 mph.

Swordfish planes flying over the *Ark Royal*

On the afternoon of May 26, the *Ark Royal* launched fifteen Swordfish torpedo planes. As they approached their target, the planes dropped their loads—only to realize at the last moment that they were actually attacking a British ship! The *Sheffield* was shadowing the Bismarck. Fortunately, the ship's captain managed to avoid the torpedoes.

At 7:30 p.m., the rearmed Swordfish planes took off again. By 8:20, they descended on the *Bismarck*. Alarms sounded all over the enormous ship. Anti-aircraft guns opened with blistering fire, but the German crew had been on station for thirty-six hours. They were exhausted.

The British pilots managed to return to the *Ark Royal* suffering no visible damage. But what the pilots couldn't see was that a torpedo had struck one of the *Bismarck*'s rudders. Remember the two rudders? They were supposed to be one of the *Bismarck*'s unique strengths. Have you ever rowed a boat with only one oar? It will only go in circles. That's exactly what happened. Instead of moving forward, the *Bismarck* with only one working rudder made one continuous turn, leaning to its port side at twelve degrees.

Repairmen struggled to fix the rudder, but the directionless ship was headed straight toward the British ships.

Admiral Lutjens sent out a radio message, "Ship unmaneuverable. We fight to the last shell. Long live the Fuehrer (Hitler)."

The *Bismarck* in flames, May 27, 1940

When the British saw the *Bismarck* in their path, they didn't realize it was there because of the rudder damage. Admiral Tovey assembled almost the entire fleet: *King George V, Prince of Wales, Dorsetshire, Rodney*, and several more ships and ordered them to open fire.

The *King George V* unleashed its weaponry.

The *Bismarck* replied, firing her 15-inch guns. But without the ability to turn, the ship was basically a sitting duck.

Soon British guns were firing full broadsides on the German ship. The *Rodney*'s shells hit and exploded on the *Bismarck*'s bridge, smashing the main gunnery and sending out a sheet of flames. Lutjens, Lindermann, and all their staff were killed.

Then the *Rodney* launched its torpedoes.

Still, the *Bismarck* kept firing. It landed a hit on the *Rodney*'s starboard side, but soon two gun turrets were destroyed on the German ship. Then a third was demolished after a shell burst inside a gun barrel. The fourth turret was disabled by another hit to a gun barrel. At 10:00 a.m., the *Bismarck*'s executive ranking officer gave the order to abandon ship. Admiral Tovey ordered all British ships with remaining torpedoes to fire on the *Bismarck*. The *Dorsetshire* scored three hits.

The *Bismarck* suddenly leaned all the way over on its side. The world's most powerful ship sank, hitting the bottom of the ocean within ten minutes.

Admiral Tovey dispatched a message to London: "I should like to pay the highest tribute for the most gallant fight put up against impossible odds, worthy of the old days of the Imperial German Navy."

Among the *Bismarck*'s 2,000-man crew, only 107 men survived.

Upon hearing this news about the *Bismarck*, Italy's foreign minister wrote in his diary, "The *Bismarck* has been sunk. This is important especially on account of the repercussions it will have in the United States, where it will prove that the seas are dominated by the Anglo-Saxons."

WHO FOUGHT?

The *Bismarck* was named for Otto von Bismarck, nicknamed the "Iron Chancellor."

Before Bismarck's rule in the 1800s, Germany consisted of thirty-nine independent states.

Bismarck started wars with Denmark, Austria, and France, and won them decisively, bringing all the states together under what was then called Prussian leadership.

"The great questions of the day," Bismarck said, "will not be settled by means of speeches and majority decisions but by iron and blood."

Bismarck was considered a master military strategist. He was also a great manipulator. He once purposefully altered a telegram from a French diplomat in order to provoke France into launching a war against Prussia.

Bismarck won that war, too.

Although he led Germany to unification, he also set the stage for both World Wars. Like Hitler, he believed the Germans were destined to rule all of Europe because they were superior. Also like Hitler, Bismarck wanted to attack Poland.

"Hit the Poles so hard that they despair of their life," he wrote in a letter to his sister. "I have full sympathy with their condition, but if we want to survive, we can only exterminate them; the wolf, too, cannot help having been created by God as he is, but people shoot him for it if they can."

It's ironic that the mighty German battleship was named for this man, since Bismarck was never interested in Germany having a navy. He believed the best way to conquer Germany's enemies was over land.

You can watch a short clip of Otto von Bismarck, probably filmed in 1890: www.firstworldwar.com/video/bismarck.htm

BOOKS

The Sinking of the Bismarck: The Deadly Hunt by William L. Shirer

World War II Warships by John Batchelor

Otto Von Bismarck: Iron Chancellor of Germany (Wicked History) by Kimberley Burton Heuston

Why Did the Whole World Go to War? And Other Questions About…World War II by Martin W. Sandler

INTERNET

YouTube offers several good films about the *Bismarck*—do a search on them.

Famed Hollywood director James Cameron documented his quest to learn more about the sunken Bismarck: www.jamescamerononline.com/Documentaries.htm

MOVIES

Sink the Bismarck!

THE BATTLE OF BRITAIN

July to November 1940

RAF pilots scramble for their planes during the Battle of Britain

WHEN THE *BISMARCK* sank to the bottom of the ocean, Germany suffered a huge loss. However, that didn't slow down Hitler.

Within weeks of the sinking, he had conquered France. Despite having one of the world's largest armies, France surrendered to Germany on June 17, 1940.

The next day, Winston Churchill stood before the British House of Commons and said, "The Battle of France is over. I expect the Battle of Britain is about to begin."

Churchill was exactly right.

Although some British politicians wanted to negotiate with

Germany, hoping to appease Hitler's lust for power, Churchill strongly disagreed. As Prime Minister of England, Churchill told his fellow countrymen that they must fight the Third Reich. If not, all of Europe would fall into another Dark Ages. In his speech, Churchill said the fight for freedom would create indescribable hardships, but free men would still say, "This was their finest hour."

With the *Bismarck* gone, Hitler couldn't invade Britain by sea. So he decided to conquer Britain by air. Just days after Churchill's stirring speech, German fighter pilots attacked England's southern coast.

The leader of the German air force, the Luftwaffe, was Hermann Goering. He told Hitler that the air force needed only one week to take down England. With 2,800 operational aircraft, the Luftwaffe would dominate England's Royal Air Force (RAF), which had only 700 fighter planes. Goering predicted that after a week of heavy aerial bombing, Germany could send in tanks and infantry, invading England, Scotland, Ireland, and Wales. Then the world would recognize Hitler's dominant forces. Every country would want to negotiate for peace with Germany.

The invasion of Britain was code named Operation Sea Lion.

Flying Messerschmitt 109s and Heinkel He 111 bombers, the Luftwaffe destroyed many southern British ports. They also hit ships traveling across the English Channel carrying war supplies.

After that first destructive wave, Germany waited for England to surrender.

But Churchill's people showed no signs of giving up. So the Luftwaffe changed tactics.

Heinkel He 111, German medium bombers

On August 15, the Germans unleashed all three air fleets—an enormous number of planes—and pummeled England. The bombings inflicted considerable damage to military communications and command centers. The attack also destroyed twenty percent of the already-struggling Royal Air Force (RAF).

But the British pilots didn't quit. Flying their Spitfires and Hawker Hurricanes, they struck back that same day, August 15, shooting down sixty German aircraft and killing 190 enemy crewmen.

The attack was so successful that Germans started calling August 15 "Black Thursday."

However, the Luftwaffe still outnumbered the RAF. If numbers won wars, Germany would've destroyed Great

Britain.

But battles aren't determined by numbers alone. Winning also requires courage, strategy, and tactics.

For courage, the British people did what Churchill asked—they fought with everything within them.

British radio put out an urgent call for volunteers, asking for all men between the ages of seventeen and sixty-five who were "able to fire a rifle or shotgun." More than one million Englishmen answered the call. Unfortunately, the country didn't have enough weapons for this part-time volunteer force, which was later named the Home Guard. So another call went out. This time for rifles. More than 20,000 rifles were donated—even the King of England gave up his entire private collection of shotguns!

For strategy and tactics, the RAF used several different plans. Sometimes they sent up one squadron and held another in reserve. Another tactic was called the Big Wing, where multiple squadrons flew up to attack the Luftwaffe. But after much debate, the Big Wing was cancelled. Britain couldn't afford to lose any more planes than necessary.

Still another tactic involved a brand-new invention called radar.

Though common today, radar was considered cutting-edge technology in 1940. The name is an acronym: **Ra**dio **D**irection **A**nd **R**anging. It works through the transmission of radio energy. The waves strike objects, pulse back as reflection, and reveal a target's position. In 1940, Britain had thirty coastal radar stations called the Chain Home System. These spots sent radar reports back to command headquarters. There were also ground observers—a corps of volunteers—who watched the skies for German planes.

A spotter with the Observer Corps watches the skies over London

The Luftwaffe kept coming, attacking mostly British air-fields, but it also destroyed a tire factory. On August 24, it bombed the city of Portsmouth and later that same night, blew up parts of London, setting the city ablaze.

In retaliation for that attack, the RAF flew out and bombed the city of Berlin, Germany.

Hitler was furious! He was not only prideful about his homeland, but his military leaders had told him the RAF planes couldn't strike Germany.

So Hitler viciously attacked England. Over the next two weeks, the Luftwaffe inflicted at least thirty heavy attacks.

Churchill continued to give passionate speeches in Parliament and over the radio, rallying his people as few leaders could. Here's one example of what Churchill said. You might want to read this aloud:

"I have nothing to offer but blood, toil, tears and sweat," Churchill told the House of Commons. "We have before us many, many long months of struggle and of suffering. You ask, what is our policy? I can say: It is to wage war, by sea, land and air, with all our might and with all the strength that God can give us; to wage war against a monstrous tyranny, never surpassed in the dark, lamentable catalogue of human crime. That is our policy. You ask, what is our aim? I can answer in one word: It is victory, victory at all costs, victory in spite of all terror, victory, however long and hard the road may be; for without victory, there is no survival."

At this time, the United States wasn't involved in this war—yet—but Churchill persuaded President Franklin Roosevelt to send supplies of ammunition, guns, tanks, and planes.

Britain also received additional help in this battle, but it wasn't intentional.

The Luftwaffe was huge and powerful, but Hitler had made one big mistake while building it. He didn't develop many long-range bombers. Germany's medium-range bombers, such as the Heinkel He 111, were only lightly armed. Germany's main fighter plane, the Messerschmitt Bf 109, could fly only limited distances. That meant German bombers didn't have much armed protection when flying toward their targets. To compensate, Goering ordered his fighter planes to stay close to the bombers. But the fighters stayed *too* close. The whole purpose of a scouting plane is to be far enough ahead to anticipate an enemy attack *before* it happens. In effect, Goering's tactic switched the Me 109s from offense to defense. That allowed the RAF, though vastly outnumbered, to shoot down more German planes. During the first six days of September alone, the RAF shot down 125 aircraft.

As the Battle of Britain progressed into autumn, the Luft-waffe continued to inflict pain. The RAF was losing its most experienced pilots and its few planes. The citizens of London began sleeping in subway tunnels to avoid the German bombings. Air raid sirens blared daily. Children were sent to the countryside for safety, leaving their parents behind in the city.

Yet the British people continued to fight.

By mid-September, the Luftwaffe decided the RAF had only 100 fighter planes left. So Germany launched a blistering daylight raid on London, hoping to eliminate the rest of the British fleet.

To their surprise, 300 British fighter planes struck back!

And yet, Hitler still didn't back down. Instead, the Luftwaffe ramped up its attacks. Following that daylight raid on London, more bombers flew in. At night, the pilots used the smoldering city fires from the first assault to find their targets in the dark.

The Germans bombed London until 4:30 the next morning.

And they kept bombing England for the next fifty-seven days straight. Day and night.

Londoners sleeping on underground train tracks and platforms during the Battle of Britain

Hitler thought that by killing as many civilians as possible, he could snuff out the steadfast British spirit. Plus he believed the near-constant destruction would create overwhelming confusion among British military leaders. Then the German forces could invade Great Britain.

But the British people were built of sterner stuff. The RAF pilots kept fighting.

In fact, Germany lost so many airplanes and pilots that Goering had to end daylight raids. By November, the Luftwaffe had lost more than 1,500 aircraft. The "one week" timeline Germany expected to conquer England had stretched into months. Yet victory was nowhere in sight. The Luftwaffe had lost more than 2,600 aircrew. Another 1,000 men were captured.

Finally, that same November, Hitler cancelled Operation Sea Lion.

Britain had won the battle.

The English paid a heavy price for this victory. Countless buildings, homes, and factories were destroyed. More than 90,000 people—most of them civilians—were casualties. The RAF lost much of its aircraft. About 1,000 of its airmen were killed or wounded.

But England's sacrifice, particularly by the RAF, had stopped Hitler's invasion.

Churchill summed up Britain's victory with these famous words: "Never in the field of human conflict was so much owed by so many to so few."

After that, the RAF pilots in the Battle of Britain were known as "The Few."

WHO FOUGHT?

Pilots of 303 (Polish) Squadron walking away from a Hawker Hurricane

During the Battle of Britain, the English were in danger of running out of fighter planes. They also didn't have enough pilots. So the RAF used pilots from other countries—New Zealand, Australia, Canada, South Africa, the United States, and Poland. There was also one Jamaican pilot.

Overall, the Polish pilots were the best fighters. But for several months, the RAF didn't use them in the battle. Why? Because the Poles didn't speak English, so the RAF couldn't tell if they actually knew how to fly an airplane!

Only when the pilot shortage became critical did the RAF form two Polish squadrons, the 302 and the 303.

Since the Poles had already fought the Germans in their homeland, these pilots had developed some tactics against the Luftwaffe. Of all the RAF units, the 303 was the top scoring, with 126 victories after only six weeks of flying.

The Americans who flew for the RAF in this battle were dubbed the Eagle Squadron. These Americans were actually prohibited by law from serving in the war, since the United States had not formally entered into the conflict. Back then, an American who defied the United States' official neutrality lost his citizenship or went to jail.

To get around that law, the Americans fighting in the Battle of Britain claimed they were from other countries already involved in the war, such as Canada. For that reason, we may never know the actual number of Americans who served in the RAF during the Battle of Britain.

However, we know that the first American airman killed in the Battle of Britain was Officer William "Billy" Fiske.

Fiske was an Olympic champion bobsledder. After his death, a memorial plaque was hung in London's St. Paul's Cathedral.

The plaque reads: "An American who died so that England might live."

BOOKS

Outbreak: 1939: The World Goes to War by Terry Charman

Battle of Britain: Cinebook Recounts by B. Asso

Churchill and the Battle of Britain: Days of Decision by Nicola Barber

First Light: The True Story of the Boy Who Became a Man in the War-Torn Skies above Britain by Geoffrey Wellum

INTERNET

Listen to Prime Minister Churchill's famous "finest hour" speech rallying the English people for the Battle of Britain: youtube.com/watch?v=G4BVzYGeF0M

Also listen to Churchill's speech on "The Few": youtu.be/Y0t-RqjMH-A

The Royal Air Force (RAF) Museum offers online exhibits, including links to the highly successful Polish pilots who helped win the Battle of Britain: www.rafmuseum.org.uk/research/online-exhibitions.aspx

MOVIES

The Battle of Britain

A Yank in the RAF

Eagle Squadron

STALINGRAD

The Battle of Two Egos

German soldiers advancing on the bombed-out city of Stalingrad

ADOLF HITLER WANTED to rule the world.

So did Josef Stalin.

They would challenge each other for power in the Battle of Stalingrad.

These two ruthless dictators launched the deadliest fight in military history, resulting in more than two million casualties.

How did it start?

About a year after the Battle of Britain, the United States

joined WWII. The Japanese had bombed Pearl Harbor, Hawaii, on December 7, 1941.

By 1942, American soldiers were fighting alongside soldiers from Britain, Australia, Canada, and New Zealand. This force was called the Allies. On the other side was the Axis, an alliance among Hitler, Mussolini's Italy, and the countries Hitler had conquered, such as Romania and Bulgaria.

You might be surprised to hear this, but during WWII the Soviet Union was part of the Allies. Soviet leader Josef Stalin was a ruthless Communist dictator, but he was fighting against Hitler. Since the Allies needed to stop Hitler, Stalin became a part of the Allies. This is another example of that old saying, "The enemy of my enemy is my friend."

By 1942, Hitler was feeling very confident. And why not? Among other countries, he'd trounced Poland, Norway, and France. German forces had also successfully invaded Russia through a battle code named Operation Barbarossa. That bloody fight killed more than three million Russians. The Nazis took another three million as prisoners.

Fortunately for Stalin, Russia had a huge population and he could still man his army. But Germany controlled one-third of the Russian railroads, forcing the country's industrial production to drop by 25 percent.

Stalin was in trouble.

In some ways, so was Hitler. Although the Germans won Operation Barbarossa, the battle cost Germany 900,000 men. It also destroyed 4,200 tanks, 100,000 trucks, and 200,000 horses.

Horses?

Are you wondering why Germany's modern mechanized army needed horses?

It was because of the Russian terrain. It was so rugged that in some places only horses could move military equipment. Another good thing about horses was that they didn't need gasoline to keep going, and Germany was running low on gasoline and oil. Hitler needed those fuels to operate all of his war machinery.

Meanwhile, the Soviet Union had plenty of oil, especially in the Caucasus region. So Hitler decided to push the Axis forces deeper into Russia and seize their oil.

Hitler hated Stalin so much that he expanded the mission's objectives. Instead of just going for the oil in the Caucasus region, Hitler decided to destroy the one Russian city named after his archenemy—Stalingrad.

Soviet T-34 tanks and a horse-drawn supply sled, southern Russia, Operation Uranus, November 1942

On June 28, 1942, Germany's powerful 6th Army attacked the Russian front line and broke through.

Stalin was in serious trouble.

For more than 700 years, Russia had held off every foreign invader. But Hitler—Stalin's archenemy!—controlled more

Russian land than any other foreigner in history.

The Soviets were still trying to recover from Operation Barbarossa. So their military tactic against the invading Germans came down to stalling. Hitler's forces would attack, the Soviets would engage for a while, then retreat. They'd attack, engage for a bit, and retreat. The Soviets repeated this process so often the Germans started to feel invincible.

"We always felt superior because the Russians went away from us and wherever they actually entered into a fight with us they were shot down," recalled Helmut Walz, a soldier with the German 305th Infantry Division in Stalingrad. "And so we did have this feeling of superiority."

When Stalin realized Hitler wanted to sack his namesake city, the Soviet dictator took it as a personal insult. Five days after the Germans turned toward Stalingrad, Stalin issued Order 227. The most famous line was: "Not one step back!"

Soviet postal stamp echoing Order 227: "Not one step back!"

Stalin demanded that every member of his Red Army—and every Soviet citizen—fight for every foot of Russian soil.

"Some not so smart people," Stalin wrote in Order 227, "comfort themselves by conversations that we can run further to the east, because we have a lot of land, many people and we'll always have plenty of bread. They use this to justify their infamous actions on the fronts... But further retreat to the east means to sentence to death our people and our Motherland, every bit of our land given to the enemy will enforce him and will weaken our defense, our Motherland."

Drumming up Russian patriotism, Stalin created penal battalions for disobedient soldiers. Battle detachments were ordered to shoot "cowards" who ran from the fight. These weren't empty threats. Stalin's secret police, the NKVD, executed more than 250,000 Red Army soldiers, and another 400,000 soldiers were sent to penal colonies.

By August, the Germans had pushed the Soviet defenders back to the suburbs of Stalingrad. By August 25, the city was officially under siege. In early September, the German steamroll began. The notorious 6th Army, with elements of the 4th Panzer Army and the carpet-bombing Luftwaffe, turned Stalingrad into dust and rubble.

But Hitler had become paranoid and distrustful of his military high command. He decided to take over and named himself Germany's new military commander. The problem was that he really didn't know what he was doing.

In October, Hitler shifted the mission's primary objective back to the Caucasus region.

Soviet soldiers (lower right) defending Stalingrad in house-to-house warfare

Stalin seized the opportunity. He'd finally realized that purging his own "coward" troops only meant losing more battles. So Stalin brought back the Soviet generals known for masterful military planning.

At the top of that list was General Georgy Zhukov. On October 14, when the Germans tried to encircle Stalingrad and cut off supplies floating down the Volga River, Zhukov held them back. Zhukov also placed Lieutenant Vasily Chuikov in charge of defending Stalingrad.

Rallying his men, Chuikov warned them that the fighting would get very dangerous, but the Soviets must hold Stalingrad at all costs. "Grab them by the belt," Chuikov said.

Two weeks later, with only one division, Chuikov counterattacked. He only managed to push the Germans back about 200 yards, but he prevented them from gaining any new territory.

With Hitler diverting his mission back to the Caucasus, his forces around Stalingrad needed to rely on other Axis troops. These soldiers—poorly trained Italians, Romanians, and Bulgarians—were no match for Stalin's renewed Red Army.

Also, the Axis troops were so deep inside the Soviet Union that their supply lines were getting stretched further and further, leaving them vulnerable to still more attacks.

Then, winter came.

Russian winters are notoriously cold and bitter. By November, the German guns were freezing and aircraft were grounded due to ice and mechanical failures.

Chuikov's stubborn stand had bought the Soviets time. The Russians quickly manufactured more tanks, aircraft, and guns. They also had another one million men, all fighting for the Motherland.

On November 19, Soviet General Nikolai Vatutin launched Operation Uranus.

First, the Red Army struck the weakest link, the Romanian defenses north of Stalingrad. The next day they attacked the Axis forces south of Stalingrad. Both Axis forces collapsed, despite help from the German 4th Panzer Army.

Vatutin's plan was brilliant. He had successfully removed the two flanks protecting the German 6th Army located deep inside Stalingrad. That allowed the Red Army to surround this "Stalingrad Pocket" and cut off all help to these elite German fighters.

Hitler's lack of expertise in military strategy showed in his response. Instead of pulling out the 6th Army, he ordered them to stay put, assuring them the Luftwaffe would drop supplies by air.

But all of Stalingrad was fighting this battle—women, children, and old people. As Chuikov predicted, the fight was mostly hand-to-hand combat.

It even moved house-to-house and room-to-room. In some instances, German soldiers were holding one floor of a building while the Soviets held the floor above or below.

The city of Stalingrad was a literal war zone.

Russian soldier helping a wounded comrade in the Battle of Stalingrad

All that street fighting wore down the Germans. Some of the strangest fights took place in city sewers. Stalin wouldn't let anyone leave the city, even as houses and apartments were destroyed. So mothers with children moved underground to escape the warfare—they actually lived in the city's sewers! But soon the fighting went underground, too, as the Soviet soldiers set traps or yanked Germans from the street.

The new front line was the most putrid part of the city.

"The Russians hid in the sewers," recalled Helmut Walz, the German infantry soldier. "If you advanced three meters, you always had to make sure and look around you to see whether they were not sitting behind you. You always had to defend yourself all around. Despite the fact we were attacking, you had to defend yourself all around."

Plus, the Soviets had snipers.

Remember during the Winter War when Finland's snipers decimated Stalin's forces so badly? After that experience, the

Soviets started using snipers, too. Propping their rifles onto crumbling windowsills inside bombed-out buildings, the Stalingrad snipers took out countless German soldiers. The most famous Stalingrad sniper was Vasily Zaitsev. In just three weeks, he killed almost 250 German soldiers.

Russian sniper in Stalingrad

For Hitler's forces, the situation was beyond grim. German General Friedrich von Paulus, commander of the 6th Army, was trapped inside Stalingrad. He knew that more than 100 miles separated his troops from the nearest German forces. So he asked Hitler for permission to abandon Stalingrad to save his men. Hitler insisted that the Luftwaffe would reach them with supplies. He ordered Paulus to stay and fight.

Paulus' men needed 500 tons of supplies daily—food, ammunition, and medicine for the wounded. Frigid December closed in, and the Luftwaffe lost 500 planes trying to drop supplies into the city. The men of the 6th Panzer struggled to survive on meager rations.

Stalingrad's citizens were also starving. Food became so scarce that people living in the sewers started eating rats and even frozen corpses.

While the Soviets planned a new offensive to finish off the 6th Army, Hitler also came up with a new idea. He ordered Field Marshall Erich von Manstein to relieve Paulus inside the city. The plan was called Operation Winter Storm.

But by December 16, the Soviets had destroyed Manstein's left flank, composed of the Italian 8th Army. Von Manstein continued to attack, but he was fighting with a shrinking force—and he was fighting in the Russian winter. The closest he came to Stalingrad was thirty-five miles outside the city lines.

Finally, Manstein informed Hitler that he couldn't relieve von Paulus.

Unless...

Unless Paulus tried to break out! Then Manstein could meet him at a halfway point.

But when a messenger was sent into Stalingrad, Paulus replied, "You are talking to dead men."

The Soviets drove Manstein all the way back to where his original attack had started. Instead of trying to break through to the 6th Army, Manstein decided to save his own men. Between January and March 1943, he performed a series of tactical maneuvers that saved most of his forces.

And Paulus?

The Soviets offered him several chances to surrender. He refused.

On January 10, more than 7,000 Soviet guns opened fire on the Germans, followed by tanks and infantry.

The Germans put up a strong resistance, but it was not enough. On January 3, von Paulus' headquarters was overrun. He was captured, and two days later, Germany surrendered the Battle of Stalingrad.

After five months, one week, and three days of fighting, more than two million people were killed, wounded, or captured.

But this battle was a crucial turning point in WWII—Hitler was on the run.

Axis prisoners of war, marching on a road near Stalingrad, Russia, circa
February, 1943

WHO FOUGHT?

Soviet snipers in WWII

When the German 16th Panzer Division moved on the Stalingrad Tractor Factory, the Soviet's 1077th regiment hit back.

The regiment had no men, only females.

Some of these girls were just out of high school. Armed with M1939 air defense guns, the young women fired on the German tanks and submachine gunners for two days. They destroyed eighty-three tanks, fifteen infantry vehicles, and killed three battalions of infantry. They also shot down fourteen aircraft.

When the Germans finally overwhelmed the regiment, they were stunned to discover only women among the dead soldiers. Women did not fight as soldiers in wars.

But during WWII, more than 2,000 Soviet women were snipers. Other Soviet women flew as fighter pilots and belonged to the Night Witches, an all-female bomber squadron that only flew at night. There in the dark, these women navigated old biplanes that weren't equipped with guns or parachutes.

During the Battle of Stalingrad, one Soviet woman named Natalya Meklin bombed German supply lines. By the end of the war, she had flown 980 successful night missions, a remarkable achievement that earned her the Hero of the Soviet Union medal.

The Soviets were the only Allied country that sent women into combat during WWII.

BOOKS

Stalingrad (Sieges That Changed the World) by Tim McNeese

Impossible Victory: The Battle of Stalingrad by Eric Fein

Finding Zasha by Randi Barrow

DK Eyewitness Books: World War II by Simon Adams

INTERNET

Listen to Helmut Walz, the German soldier with the 305th Infantry Division, as he describes the house-to-house fighting in Stalingrad: ww2history.com/testimony/Eastern/German_soldier_Stalingrad

Want to see what the "sewer fighting" was like? Here's a short scene from the movie *Stalingrad*: youtube.com/watch?v=-8v62cNc1vc

Truly remarkable photos from WWII's eastern front: www.theatlantic.com/photo/2011/09/world-war-ii-the-eastern-front/100150

MOVIES

Stalingrad

THE SCHNELLBOOT AND THE PT BOAT

Early PT Boat. Notice the two torpedoes on this side and the twin .50 caliber machine guns.

THE FAMOUS QUESTION asks: Which came first, the chicken or the egg?

In terms of naval warfare, that same question might be: Which came first, the torpedo or the torpedo boat?

The answer is: the torpedo.

An Englishman named Robert Whitehead invented the torpedo in 1868. But it was another ten years before a torpedo was fired—when a Russian steamer ship sank a Turkish steamer.

That sinking convinced several European countries that they should invest in torpedoes. Rather than retrofit their existing warships to fire these weapons, military leaders wanted to build specific boats. In 1900, the cost of building one battleship was the same as building sixty torpedo boats.

In the decades leading up to WWII, two of the greatest torpedo boats known to man were invented—the *Schnellboot* and the Patrol Torpedo boat, also known as the PT boat.

A *Schnellboot* slices the waves at full speed. Note the cannon fixed on the bow.

Remember how the Treaty of Versailles placed restrictions on Germany and how Hitler thumbed his nose at those rules? One of those restrictions was that Germany couldn't build any naval ships.

But Germany secretly worked around those restrictions. For instance, during the 1930s, Hitler sent his military officers into the Soviet Union to help train Stalin's troops. Although these two dictators hated each other, the arrangement was one of those *you-scratch-my-back-I'll-scratch-yours* situations. In exchange for training the Soviet troops, Germany was allowed to manufacture military equipment on Soviet land. So, technically, Hitler could claim Germany itself wasn't making weapons.

That was how the amazing *Schnellboot* was built.

Nicknamed the *S-boot*, this vessel was designed like a speedboat, 115 feet in length and sporting an engine with 2,500 horsepower, capable of speeds up to 43.8 knots—about 50.4 miles per hour, as one knot equals 1.150 mph.

With its wood-and-alloy frame, the *S-boot* maneuvered on the open sea better than other small craft. Its angled rudders could be tilted up to 30 degrees, creating an air pocket that lifted the boat so that it almost hydroplaned across the water. Lifting it like that also reduced the boat's wake, or waves, making it that much harder for an enemy to spot the vessel, especially at night.

An armored bridge protected the command center. Torpedo tubes were set internally, loaded with four torpedoes. Other armaments varied, but the *S-boot* always had 2 cm-cannons on its bow (or front) and twin 2 cm-flak guns, along with a rack of depth charges.

Ironically, it was the restrictions in the Treaty of Versailles that gave Germany the idea for this boat. It wasn't supposed to build any large warships, so its engineers designed a powerful speedboat. In the German language, "schnell" means "fast."

Fortunately for the Allies, they also had a fast boat—the Patrol Torpedo boat or PT boat.

PT boats racing at high speed. Note the torpedoes on sides.

The first PT boat was actually manufactured during WWI. But America's military leaders didn't think the original design was good enough. So the PT boats were sold to other countries, including Italy. Meanwhile, America's naval yards continued to build large destroyers.

In the 1930s, America had interests in the Philippine Islands, and suddenly the patrol boat design looked like a good tool for coastal defenses. In 1938, several boat builders entered a PT competition. The entries were numbered *PT-1* through *PT-19*. The navy tested them, but once again decided the vessels weren't up to military standards.

Then in 1941, the Electric Launch Company (Elco) came up with *PT-20*.

Seventy-seven feet long, this boat weighed thirty-three tons and carried four torpedoes, eight depth charges, and two dual .50 caliber machine guns. With three engines, this wooden vessel could quickly reach speeds of 41 knots.

When the Japanese bombed Pearl Harbor, Hawaii, the PT boat hit the ocean.

These vessels had a crew of two officers and ten enlisted

men. As the war progressed, the PT boats started carrying smaller but more powerful torpedoes. Sometimes they also had radar. The PTs attacked cruisers, destroyers, submarines, and supply barges. They covered a diverse area, from the South Pacific to the Mediterranean Sea, from the English Channel to the Aleutian Islands of Alaska.

In the Pacific, these buccaneers of the sea destroyed hundreds of barges loaded with Japanese troops and supplies. Quick and agile, the PTs slipped inside enemy harbors, conducted sabotage and raiding missions behind enemy lines, and rescued aircrews whose planes went down at sea.

They did it all while shooting against massive coastal guns and ships that were 100 times their size. The speedy PTs would zigzag across the water, dodging enemy fire. They were so fast that American squadrons started calling the PTs "the mosquito fleet."

But the Japanese, who struggled to sink them and who suffered many losses because of them, called the PTs "Devil Boats."

WHO FOUGHT?

PT-109 in the South Pacific

On a moonless August night in 1943, Lieutenant John F. Kennedy and his crew were quietly idling in the South Pacific Ocean aboard *PT-109*. The crew was trying to avoid detection by Japanese aircraft. Around 2:00 a.m., the crew suddenly realized that a fast-moving Japanese destroyer was heading straight for them.

Before the crew could fire up the engines, the destroyer sliced *PT-109* in half.

And yet, the mighty little boat kept going—half floating, half sinking. After several hours at sea, Kennedy, the crew's leader, decided their best chance of survival was to swim for some nearby islands. Since the Japanese had prison camps on the larger islands, the crew headed for a small island. They placed lanterns, shoes, and men who couldn't swim onto the wood that was once the boat's gun mount.

They swam for hours. Some of the men had been badly injured when the destroyer hit them and couldn't swim. Kennedy was an expert swimmer. He towed one enlisted man over three miles—by clenching the man's life vest strap between his teeth. Once they reached the island, Kennedy and ten surviving men lived on coconut milk and rainwater. Days later, some island natives discovered them and offered shelter. Each night, Kennedy would send out signals, hoping to make contact with any American naval ships in the area.

Six days later, the crew of *PT-109* was rescued by another PT boat. Kennedy was later awarded military honors for his courage and leadership.

In 1960, Kennedy became the 35th president of the United States.

BOOKS

PT Boats in Action Warships No. 34 by David Doyle

John F. Kennedy and PT-109 by Richard Tregaskis

ELCO 80 PT Boat On Deck Color Series No. 5 by David Doyle

Higgins PT Boats On Deck by David Doyle

INTERNET

Here's a YouTube video of the only operational PT boat still in existence: youtube.com/watch?v=ucciZ1zFpXY

Here is a longer video on the history and use of the PT boat during WWII: youtube.com/watch?v=FtMJFROT2zk

See the world's last surviving *S-Boot*: www.bmpt.org.uk/boats/S130/index1.htm

MOVIES

They Were Expendable PT 109

OPERATION TORCH

Nov. 8–10, 1942

American troops hit a beach near Algiers on November 8, 1942

"A HOUSE DIVIDED against itself cannot stand." Abraham Lincoln said that right before the United States entered the American Civil War.

Nearly 100 years later, Lincoln's words still rang true all the way across the other side of the globe.

During WWII, France was a divided country. After the country surrendered to Hitler on June 17, 1940, some French leaders believed that by offering Hitler a good deal, he would leave them alone. Other leaders wanted to keep fighting Germany.

Then France literally divided itself in half. It offered the northern part to Germany, while the southern half supposedly remained "independent French." But the southern French leader, Henri Pétain, sympathized with Hitler. Since Pétain's government was headquartered in the small town of Vichy, people started using the term "Vichy French" to mean *French-but-really-controlled-by-Hitler*.

The map below shows how France was divided after its surrender to Germany.

However, Hitler wasn't satisfied with ownership of half of France—he wanted to control all of Europe. By 1942, Germany controlled all of France. The Nazis ordered the French to arrest and deport all its Jewish citizens. These people were sent to concentration camps. The Nazis also controlled the entire French army. Most of France's supplies went to the Nazis. French citizens had such a hard time getting gasoline that they started fueling their trucks with charcoal and wood pellets. Leather became so rare that French people soled their shoes with wood. When the Germans seized all of the food and its production, hunger spread. In the cities, people starved. On the farms, they hid cows, chickens, and pigs from the Germans for survival.

By controlling France, Hitler now ruled from the Arctic Circle to the deserts of Egypt, from the French coasts along the Atlantic Ocean to the Eastern shore of the Black Sea in Russia.

Seeing Hitler's spread of power, Josef Stalin begged the Allies to invade Europe. An Allied invasion would force Germany to shift troops away from the Russian Front. Then Stalin could reorganize his forces.

But in 1942, the United States had only been fighting in the war for about a year. America was still trying to train troops, manufacture war supplies, and fight the relentless Japanese forces in the Pacific. America couldn't afford to invade Europe and hope to win—especially when Hitler had the "home field advantage."

So the Allies devised another way to fight Hitler. They decided to invade another area that would divert Hitler's focus.

Look at the map below. The Mediterranean Sea washes up against southern France and Spain. Across the water is North Africa, where the countries of Tunisia, Morocco, and Algeria were French colonies. With the current state of affairs in Vichy France, the North African countries were occupied by Nazi troops.

The Allies decided to invade North Africa.

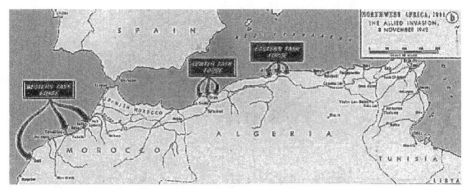

Main landing areas for Operation Torch in North Africa

Code named Operation Torch, this invasion was led by American General Dwight Eisenhower (who would later become president of the United States). In early November 1942, more than 600 ships carried 70,000 Allied troops to Morocco and Algeria.

Initially, the invasion saw no real resistance. Eisenhower even started negotiating surrender with Vichy France, since the French now realized that "appeasing" Hitler meant giving Hitler everything he demanded. Within days, Eisenhower convinced Vichy France to join the Allied forces in North Africa.

This quick victory gave the Allies a false sense of confidence.

The German forces, named the Afrika Korps, were among the most highly trained troops in the world, led by a truly brilliant military tactician, General Erwin Rommel. Even Rommel's enemies respected him. Additional German forces were fighting in North Africa under General Jürgen von Arnim, along with some fairly well-trained Italian forces.

Soon after the invasion, these Axis forces began crushing the Allies.

German vehicles of 21st Panzer Division on the move in North Africa, 1942

Many of the American troops landing in North Africa's sand-stormed deserts had no combat experience. They didn't know how to use their weapons—including bazookas and land mines—and they couldn't tell enemy forces from friendly ones. They also weren't trained to fight at night.

Meanwhile, the experienced Germans were using classic Blitzkrieg maneuvers, forcing the panicked Allies to retreat. Sometimes the German tanks retreated, too. The Americans would chase them—only to discover they were trapped by German anti-tank 88mm guns waiting for their arrival.

"It was murder," recalled one American artillery soldier who served in North Africa. The Allied tanks "rolled right into the muzzles of the concealed eighty-eights and all I could do was stand by and watch tank after tank blown to bits or burst into flames or just stop, wrecked."

Inexperienced American soldiers also dug shallow slit trenches in the desert soil instead of deep foxholes. German tanks started rolling over these hiding spots, then making a half-turn on top, crushing every man beneath the armored vehicle's treads. It's difficult to name all the individual battles in North Africa. But among the most significant were several battles at Kasserine Pass, Tunisia. Among them, the Battle of Sidi Bou Zid revealed the fatal flaws in the Allied forces.

British Major General Lloyd Fredendall was leading the battle, but he'd never been in combat himself. During the campaign for North Africa, Fredendall stayed inside headquarters, consulting maps to locate his troops. Fredendall never once visited the front lines. He even ordered 200 engineers to build him a concrete bunker located many, many miles away from the front lines.

An American M3 Grant tank near Kasserine Pass in Tunisia, late February, 1943

In the Battle of Sidi Bou Zid, Fredendall ordered his troops onto two hills that flanked a main road headed into Kasserine

Pass. On each hill, he placed an infantry regiment and a company of tanks. Unfortunately, Fredendall's maps didn't show how far apart these hills were. Essentially Fredendall's placement created two isolated outposts.

On February 14 at 6:30 a.m., 100 German tanks barreled through Kasserine Pass, surrounded each hill, and split the Allied forces.

In a counterattack, Fredendall sent in fifty tanks and tank destroyers and told them to charge forward. However, he placed the tanks in a tight parade pattern, lined up like toy soldiers—no concealment, no flanking protection. The Germans struck them down like bowling pins.

The Allied Sherman tanks had one advantage over the German tanks. Shermans came equipped with a 75 mm gun. The German Panzer III only had a 50 mm gun. But Rommel's tactical brilliance wiped out that advantage. Outmaneuvering the Shermans, the Panzers aimed for the enemy's gas tanks, blowing up the armored vehicles. If the remaining Allied troops went into reverse, seeking safety, the German artillery was waiting for them.

The next day, about 1,900 Allied infantrymen were still stuck on those ridges. The 1st Armored Division arrived as a relief force, but not having learned the lesson from the day before, they went in with the exact same tactics.

The Germans destroyed forty-six of the fifty tanks.

That night, what remained of the American troops attempted to escape through German lines.

More than 1,400 men were captured.

The battle lasted ten days. The Germans pushed the Americans back fifty miles, destroyed 183 tanks, killed 300 men, captured 4,000 men, and another 3,000 were missing.

General Eisenhower learned critical lessons from this battle. He replaced the weaker Allied leaders and ordered command centers to be located near the front lines.

He also brought in General George S. Patton.

General George S. Patton in North Africa, wearing his customary uniform of jodhpurs and boots, pointing his riding crop

Joined by Vichy French troops, the Allied forces moved toward the Atlas Mountains of Tunisia. Rommel had planned to push the Allies into the dry rocky steppes to keep them from getting to the Mediterranean Sea and hitting German supply lines. Rommel also wanted to resupply his own troops by capturing an Algerian depot that belonged to the Allies.

If Rommel's plan had worked, the battle in North Africa would've turned out differently.

But the Allied forces were now led by General Patton. They powered through Tunisia's mountain passes while Allied planes and ships destroyed Axis transport aircraft and fighters.

Rommel also had another problem. He and fellow general Arnim hated each other. Since the German field commander couldn't decide which general was actually in charge, the Nazis wasted two weeks bickering about their next move.

During that time, the Allies regrouped.

By April, American, British, and Australian forces, along with some New Zealanders of Maori descent, captured German-held airfields and ports.

On April 18, 1943, forty-seven P-40s and twelve Spitfire fighter planes intercepted an Axis convoy off Tunisia and shot down twenty-four German transport aircraft and more than a dozen fighter planes. So many troops were lost that the Germans referred to that day as the Palm Sunday Massacre.

By the end of April, the Luftwaffe began evacuating Axis troops.

In May, the Allies controlled most of North Africa, and Rommel was forced to leave the battlefront due to poor health.

Operation Torch had worked—the Allies had successfully attacked Hitler's forces.

However, Hitler still controlled Europe, and he was already anticipating the Allies' next move.

English Prime Minister Winston Churchill knew this, too. "Every bloody fool knows Sicily is next," he complained.

Sicily is an island just off the southern coast of Italy across the Mediterranean Sea. The Allies needed Hitler to think they were going to attack somewhere else. To fool him, they needed a trick.

A very convincing trick.

So began the top-secret mission called Operation Mincemeat.

WHO FOUGHT?

During the battles of North Africa, General Erwin Rommel was nicknamed "The Desert Fox" for his sly maneuvers that used the element of surprise.

Rommel often placed his forces where nobody expected them. He saw the desert as an ocean, with his artillery tanks sailing across the sand like ships. Rommel's Panzer division was so fast it earned the nickname the "Ghost Division" because it moved so quickly that even German commanders lost track of it.

Rommel was among Hitler's closest advisors. But Rommel was not like most Nazi officers. His Afrika Korps was never accused of war crimes. Rommel also treated captured soldiers humanely, even cutting his own troops' water rations in order to provide water for prisoners of war (POWs). Remarkably, Rommel ignored the orders of the Gestapo—the German police—to kill all Jewish soldiers and civilians.

Rommel also changed his mind about Germany's leader and was linked to a conspiracy to assassinate Hitler. When Hitler found out, he immediately wanted to kill Rommel. But the German general was a national hero. So Hitler offered Rommel a deal—if he committed suicide, the Nazis wouldn't kill Rommel's family.

On October 14, 1944, Erwin Rommel swallowed a cyanide pill. Minutes later, he was dead. The German people were told that Rommel died when enemy forces strafed his car in France. Rommel was given a state funeral with full honors.

BOOKS

Desert Rat 1940-43: British and Commonwealth Troops in North Africa by Tim Moreman and Steve Noon

Spitfire Aces of North Africa and Italy (Aircraft of the Aces) by Andrew Thomas and Chris Davey

Operation Torch: Anglo-American Invasion of North Africa by Vincent Jones

An Army at Dawn: The War in North Africa, 1942-43 by Rick Atkinson

Meeting the Fox: The Allied Invasion of Africa, from Operation Torch to Kasserine Pass to Victory in Tunisia by Orr Kelly

Assault From The Sea: Amphibio by Tom Mcgowen

The Good Fight: How World War II Was Won by Stephen E. Ambrose

INTERNET

More details on Blitzkrieg:
www.historylearningsite.co.uk/blitzkrieg.htm

Great photos and details about the US Rangers involved with Operation Torch: airgroup4.com/operation-torch.htm

Watch a newsreel from the 1940s, showing the invasion of North
     Africa: www.wwiireels.com

Search the amazing WWII photos, stories, profiles and more at
     ww2db.com

MOVIES

The Big Red One Desert Fox Desert Rats

OPERATION MINCEMEAT

The spies who planned Operation Mincemeat: Lt. Charles Cholmondeley, left, and Ewen Montagu, right. April 1943

YOU'VE PROBABLY HEARD of James Bond, the movie spy known as "007." Working for the British government, Bond used all kinds of cool gadgets against the bad guys.

During WWII, the author who created James Bond, Ian Fleming, worked inside Britain's spy agency. Fleming was there when British spies devised a plan against Hitler's troops. It sounded just like a James Bond adventure, but it was real— Operation Mincemeat.

When the Allies took control of North Africa, both sides figured the next stop would be Sicily. Look at the map. The island of Sicily sits just off the Italian mainland, near the "toe" of Italy's "boot." From there, Allied forces could hop into Italy and start fighting Hitler in Europe.

But if the Axis forces knew the Allied invasion was coming, they would beef up their resistance. So the Allies wanted to fool Hitler into thinking the invasion wasn't at Sicily.

The Germans, however, were suspicious of nearly everything. So this plan had to be a very good trick. The Allies called in two excellent spies: Lieutenant Charles Cholmondeley (pronounced "Chumly") and Ewen Montagu. These men came up with a plan that began with a dead body. A thirty-four-year-old homeless man had died after swallowing rat poison. His name was Glyndwr Michael. He had no living relatives, no known friends, and his death went unnoticed by everyone— except the spies in British counterintelligence.

The spies created a new identity for Glyndwr Michael. In death, he became British Major William "Bill" Martin of the Royal Marines. They invented his family and gave him an impressive education, along with the best clothing money could buy—nice clothing was rare during the war.

Major Martin was also engaged to be married. His fiancé, Pam, wrote love letters to Major Martin. In reality, these letters were written by a female employee in the spy department. The spies placed these letters inside a briefcase, which also held a receipt for Pam's diamond engagement ring.

Photograph of "Pam" placed inside "Major Martin's" briefcase. This woman, Jean Leslie, worked with the spies on Operation Mincemeat.

The briefcase also held a book of stamps, some keys, one pencil, one silver cross, and a note from the bank about an overdraft. The spies added theater tickets and a hotel bill from London—all printed on real stationary showing the dates that Major Martin was in London.

Then came the really important documents: "official" top-secret letters, written in code. The documents explained how the Allies planned to invade…Greece.

Check your map. Greece sits some distance to the east from Sicily.

To make the invasion of Greece seem even more real, the official documents named which troops were assigned to the mission and which beaches they would hit. There was even a second phase to the invasion, called Operation Brimstone. The note said, "We stand a very good chance of making [the Germans] think we are going for Sicily."

Pretty tricky, huh?

Since real people make mistakes, the spies added some errors to the documents. For instance, they made it look like Major Martin once lost his military identification card, and that he forgot to renew his officer's pass for headquarters.

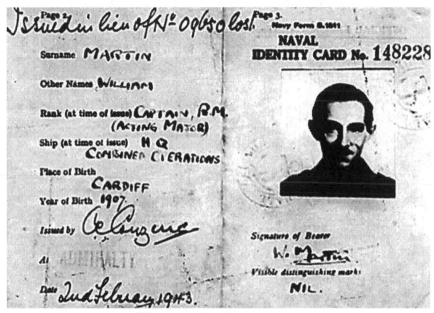

Major Martin's "official" identification card

These "mistakes" were risky. The Germans might wonder why somebody so careless would be trusted with official secrets. On the other hand, if there were no mistakes, would Major Martin seem real?

When all the paperwork was completed, Major Martin's body was placed in a sealed steel canister wearing a Royal Marines uniform. The canister was filled with dry ice to preserve the body.

The British submarine HMS *Seraph* carried the canister to the coast of Spain. On April 30, the Seraph's commander Lieutenant Bill Jewell gathered his officers on deck and finally explained this top-secret mission. Opening the canister, the crew gave Major Martin a life jacket, chained the briefcase around his waist like a bank official trying to prevent theft, and then read aloud the Bible's 39th Psalm which begins, "I said, I will take heed to my ways…"

Then Major Martin was launched out to sea.

Hours later, a local Spanish fisherman found the body. He turned it over to law enforcement. A Spanish pathologist (a doctor who examines dead bodies) concluded that this British officer probably died in an airplane crash at sea.

Back in London, British spy Montagu placed Major Martin's name in the daily newspaper under the listing of British casualties—just in case the Germans checked. Amazingly, that same day two British officers really did die in a plane crash in that same area!

Below you can read the newspaper notice. See the last line under "Officers, Killed."

ROYAL NAVY

The Board of Admiralty regrets to announce the following casualties which have been sustained in meeting the general hazards of war.   Next-of-kin have been notified:—

OFFICERS

KILLED

A/Capt. Sir T. L. Beevor, Bt:. R.N.; T/Lt. D. A. Burgass, R.N.V.R.; Lt. J. L. Fraser, R.N.V.R.; Lt. P. F. S. Gould,' D.S.C., R.N.; T/Sub-Lt. (A) J. H. Hodgson, R.N.V.R.; T/Sub-Lt. (A) K. R. Joll, R.N.V.R.; Rear-Admiral P. J. Mack, D.S.O.; T/Lt (A) G. Muttrie, R.N.V.R.; T/Lt. (A) G. Raynor, R.N.V.R.; T/Sub-Lt. J. N. Wishart, R.N.V.R.
ROYAL MARINES.—T/Capt (A/Major) W. Martin.

DIED FROM WOUNDS OR INJURIES

T/Sub-Lt. (A) J. Hall, R.N.V.R.; T/Lt. A. G. D. Heybyrne, R.N.V.R.

The plan seemed to be going well, until Major Martin's briefcase got "lost."

The Brits suspected it was taken by the Spanish or German government. So they pretended to be *very* interested in recovering those papers—just enough that the Germans didn't suspect it was a trick.

In actuality, the Spanish Navy had taken the briefcase and turned it over to a higher authority.

After that, it really did "disappear." Even the Nazis couldn't find it.

Hearing the Brits wanted the briefcase, suddenly the Germans *really* wanted to find it. They convinced Spain to hand over the documents. Spanish authorities had managed to remove the still-damp paper from its envelope without breaking the wax seal. How? By inserting a slender probe under the sealed flap, winding the paper into a cylinder, and carefully pulling it out.

The "official" documents were taken to the German Embassy in Spain where they were copied and replaced in their original envelopes, by reversing the removal process.

With everything inside, the briefcase was returned to the British.

But spies are spies. Even though the envelopes were never opened, British counterintelligence could tell that the documents had been removed and read.

That was good news.

Unfortunately, one person doubted all this information—Joseph Goebbels, the Nazi minister of propaganda. Goebbels knew it could be a trick. After all, before the invasion of Poland, Goebbels had helped fool the world about those Polish spies at the radio station. But Goebbels only voiced his doubts inside his private diary, and never said anything to Hitler, who was totally convinced that Major Martin had been a real British officer carrying authentic documents.

So Germany moved its defensive forces from Sicily to Greece, along with the masterful General Rommel, three Panzer divisions, and many mines and minesweepers.

Hearing this news, the British spies sent a secret message to Churchill. It read, "Mincemeat Swallowed Whole."

Now the Allies would head for Sicily.

WHO FOUGHT?

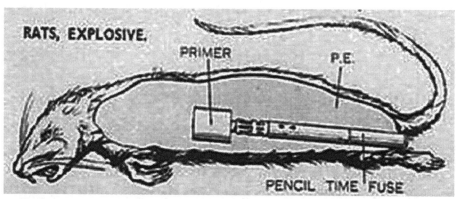

Explosives were placed inside rat skins, sewn up, and spread around factories. When the "dead rat" was thrown into the factory broiler's fire, it would explode, destroying the factory.

Rats—exploding rats!

Buttons that were compasses.

Tobacco pipes that turned into guns.

These gadgets were among the highly inventive tools created by British counterintelligence during WWII. Spies also built radios that looked like ordinary objects. One radio looked just like an English biscuit tin and was parachuted into France to help the Resistance that was secretly fighting German occupation.

Even if the electricity went out and there weren't any batteries, the radio would still work because the spies also created a bicycle that generated electricity when pedaled. That electricity could be stored in a generator for later use.

Another popular gizmo was the spike letterbox. It looked like an ordinary iron road spike, except it was hollow and could hold secret messages placed along roads and fence posts.

Even clotheslines played a role in counterintelligence. A row of clothing hanging on the line in this order might send a message: **H**andkerchief, **e**iderdown, **l**ace, and **p**ants spelled **HELP**.

BOOKS

Ultra Hush-hush: Espionage and Special Missions (Outwitting the Enemy: Stories from World War II) by Stephen Shapiro, Tina Forrester, and David Craig

Operation Mincemeat: How a Dead Man and a Bizarre Plan Fooled the Nazis and Assured an Allied Victory by Ben Macintyre

INTERNET

The British Broadcasting Company produced a documentary about Operation Mincemeat. This web page will take you to the hour-long show: bbc.co.uk/programmes/b00wllmb

Read more about WWII's British spy gadgets and spies here: www.warhistoryonline.com/war-articles/crafty-gadgets-tricks-famous-wwii-spies.html

The History Channel has a short video that shows some clever WWII spy tricks: history.com/topics/world-war-ii/world-war-ii-history/videos/wwii-spy-strategy

Want to see even more gadgets, including some from the modern era? nbcnews.com/id/38057753/ns/technology_and_science-science/t/trickiest-spy-gadgetsever/#.U864JijLKZg

Check out the International Spy Museum in Washington DC by visiting online: www.spymuseum.org

MOVIES

The Man Who Never Was

OPERATION HUSKY

The Invasion of Sicily, July 9– August 17, 1943

The *SS Robert Rowan* explodes after being hit by a German bomber during Operation Husky. July 11, 1943

CHURCHILL CALLED ITALY the "soft underbelly of Europe" because it seemed like the easiest way to sneak into Europe. Hitler's Italian divisions were poorly trained, but now they also hated their dictator Benito Mussolini.

However, the invasion of Italy wasn't easy.

Code named Operation Husky, the invasion was supposed to have the Allied Forces land on the northwest and southeast coasts of Sicily. The British 8th Army was led by General Bernard Montgomery, and General Patton led the 7th Army. In front of both of them was the 82nd Airborne led by Colonel James Gavin.

The airborne troops saw the first sign of trouble. In the early morning hours of July 10, more than 3,000 paratroopers were flown from Tunisia in northern Africa and dropped into Sicily. These airborne units were supposed to help secure the main beachhead landings and protect the assault troops. But high winds, poor navigation, and inexperienced pilots ruined the drop. It turned into a fiasco. Only about 100 paratroopers landed near their intended zone. The other 2,900 men were scattered across the island.

Colonel Gavin, landing with his men, realized they'd missed their drop. In the distance, he saw bursting shells. "And we were moving toward the sound of the guns," he later said, "one of the first battle axioms I had learned as a cadet at West Point." Gavin was about twenty miles east of his drop zone. He and his small band walked all night, running into their first firefight as they came up against an Italian patrol unit. After some fierce fighting, Gavin and his men escaped, with Gavin making sure he was the last man to withdraw.

Ironically, the invasion's ruined drop worked in the Allies' favor. Scattered far and wide, the paratroopers were forced to fight independently and take on the enemy using basic guerrilla tactics—from cutting communication wires to ambushing German and Italian patrols. The Axis forces, seeing all these fighters, fell into complete confusion. Reports started going into headquarters describing a large number of paratroopers roaming Sicily's hills and valleys.

The Axis forces assumed two Allied divisions had landed in Sicily, believing there were many thousands of soldiers instead of the actual three thousand.

The next morning, Gavin and his men headed for the town of Guila. He found 200 more Allied men and formed a platoon with the 307th Combat Engineers. Continuing toward the town, he heard gunfire coming from a ridge that overlooked a river, later known as Biazza Ridge.

Gavin and his men had run into a German division fighting the American 108th Infantry. Taking the lead, Gavin with his platoon attacked and took the ridge. They held it without help of armor or artillery, but the Germans regrouped and pinned them on the ridge under heavy rifle and machine gun fire. Gavin called up his 3rd Battalion for reinforcements. They attacked across the base of the ridge, while Gavin and his men charged down the hill, joining the attack.

Together they pushed back the Germans.

Guess who was in that fierce 3rd Battalion force? Cooks. Clerks. Orderlies. They were the only men available.

British Sherman tank of the Eighth Army in the streets of Sicily, July, 1943

After getting pushed down the slope, the Germans counter-attacked with mortars, artillery, and machine gun fire. Gavin and his men retreated over the crest of the ridge, and found H Company. These men fixed bayonets to their rifles and charged right back over the ridge, fighting the Germans in hand-to-hand combat, killing until the enemy retreated.

Immediately following this battle, they had to face another German counterattack. This time the Germans attacked with Tiger tanks. Twenty-seven feet long and weighing about sixty tons, these tanks were armed with an 88mm cannon and two machine guns.

The Allies had nothing to compare with that kind of power.

But Gavin had included some 75mm howitzers in his drop supplies. He put these artillery guns to good use. Right as the Tigers crested the ridge to open fire on the Americans, Gavin aimed the howitzers at the Tigers' underbellies. The attack slowed the German assault, but by 4:00 p.m., the Tigers were still pushing forward and had come only fifty yards from Gavin's command post.

The situation didn't look hopeful.

Gavin's radiomen made contact with the American naval fleet that was stationed off Sicily's coast. These ships directed their 150mm cannons toward the German Tigers and fired, forcing the Germans to retreat.

At 7:00 p.m., with Gavin's forces still holding the ridge, the 45th Infantry Division arrived with fifty men and some Sherman tanks. Gavin decided to attack once more.

The Americans held the ridge.

Historian Clay Blair has called this ridge battle "one of the finest, most dogged displays of leadership in all of WWII."

By holding the high ground above the water, Gavin's forces allowed the 1st Division to land on its beachhead without heavy enemy fire. Soon after, Gavin became the youngest major general of WWII, at age thirty-seven.

Along Sicily's southeastern shore, Patton's army moved up the coast, then turned east toward the town of Messina to protect Montgomery's flank of veteran forces, which were coming from the northwest.

The Germans, having swallowed the bait from Operation Mincemeat, still didn't have a large force assembled in Italy. Hitler remained convinced that the real Allied invasion was still coming—in Greece. In fact, it was another two weeks before Hitler figured out the trick.

By then, Italy's fascist government was falling apart under the Allied invasion. Mussolini was deposed (removed from his office) and arrested. The new Italian government opposed Hitler's Nazis and started talking to the Allies about an armistice, or peace agreement. The day after Mussolini's arrest, Italian troops began withdrawing from Sicily.

However, Hitler's forces continued to fight, forcing Patton's and Montgomery's armies to struggle. The Germans knew Sicily's rough terrain like the back of their hands. Then on August 17, Patton's troops closed in on the town of Messina. The Allies had managed to trap most of the Germans in this northeast corner of the island. Patton expected a horrendous fight.

Yet when the Allies pushed into Messina, every German was gone.

Under cover of darkness, Germany had evacuated about 100,000 men, along with vehicles, supplies, and ammunition.

Operation Husky was finished. It was an Allied victory, but it resulted in more than 23,000 Allied casualties.

The Italian mainland still lay ahead, which would lead to some of the most difficult campaigns of WWII.

WHO FOUGHT?

James Maurice Gavin was the youngest American general of WWII. He was known as "The Jumping General" because he jumped with the combat paratroopers under his command. A great leader, Gavin was awarded many distinguished medals for his courage and success.

Gavin's life didn't start out great.

At age two, he was placed in a New York orphanage. Although a couple from Pennsylvania later adopted him, the family struggled financially. In the eighth grade, Gavin dropped out of school to work as a shoe clerk. When he was seventeen, he ran away from home, but he sent a telegram to his parents, telling them he was in New York City.

That same year, 1924, Gavin lied to a US Army recruiting officer, saying he was an eighteen-year-old orphan. Gavin knew his adoptive parents would never consent to his enlisting in the army. The recruiting officer took Gavin to a lawyer who legally declared the officer his guardian, allowing the officer to sign Gavin's consent forms.

As an eighth-grade dropout, Gavin made up for lost learning by reading books, including biographies of great military leaders. A sergeant recognized the boy's potential and made Gavin his assistant. Six months later, Gavin was promoted to corporal. He then applied to a local army school, working daily with a tutor to pass the entrance exams for West Point Military Academy.

Once again, he lied. His West Point application said he was twenty-one—he was actually eighteen. Since his education didn't match his peers, Gavin got up every morning at 4:30 to read his books, sitting in the bathroom because it was the only place with enough light.

After graduation, he was commissioned as a second lieutenant.

A few years later, Gavin was ordered back to West Point where he worked in the Tactics Faculty. He began analyzing everything from Stonewall Jackson's strategies during the Civil War to the current German use of Blitzkrieg. He also realized that the American military was missing something.

"From what we had seen so far," he wrote, "it was clear the most promising area of all was airborne warfare, bringing the parachute troops and the glider troops to the battlefield in masses, especially trained, armed and equipped for that kind of warfare."

In April of 1941, Gavin was posted to a new airborne unit. Later that year, when the United States entered the war, Gavin's unit would see plenty of combat.

For his actions on the battlefield, Gavin would be awarded the Distinguished Service Cross with Oak Leaf Cluster, the Distinguished Service Medal, the Silver Star, and the Purple Heart.

The British also awarded him the Distinguished Service Order.

BOOKS

Sicily 1943: The debut of Allied joint operations by Steven Zaloga

Salerno 1943: The Allies invade southern Italy by Angus Konstam

The Good Fight: How World War II Was Won by Stephen E. Ambrose

Fortress Malta: An Island Under Siege, 1940–43 by James Holland

The Day of Battle: The War in Sicily and Italy, 1943–1944 by Rick Atkinson

INTERNET

Watch one of the historic newsreels that explained Operation Husky to the American public: youtube.com/watch?v=xo6obLzIKFg

Rare combat footage of an A-36A fighter-bomber squadron in action in Sicily—in color: youtube.com/watch?v=7HxDQdIZYoE

The War Department produced this film to familiarize American troops with the actual sound and performance of various German automatic weapons, which were used in places like Sicily: youtube.com/watch?v=oQwRjZByaok

B-17: THE FLYING FORTRESS

B-17F and the 401st Bomb Squadron flying over France. Notice the "blisters" protruding from the plane's nose, belly, and top.

DURING WORLD WAR I, soldiers fought from trenches. Each side would climb out of the ground and try to gain the "no-man's-land" between the trenches. It was a brutal method of warfare. Battlefields became drenched in blood.

When airplanes came along, men were no longer stuck fighting on the ground. Bombers could swoop over enemy territory and drop explosive bombs. The world's major powers realized that the next war would be won by whichever country had the best planes, especially bomber planes. However, since fighter planes could shoot bombers out of the sky, the winning side also needed a plane so strong and so powerful that it could carry a massive bomb load *and* defend itself against enemy fire.

That plane was the B-17, nicknamed "The Flying Fortress."

"Without the B-17, we might have lost the war," declared General Carl Spaatz, commander of the American Strategic Air Forces in Europe.

The B-17 first appeared in 1935, when the Army Air Force held a competition for aircraft manufacturers. The Boeing Company entered an innovative airplane that had gone from the design board to test flight in just twelve months.

Labeled XB-17 (X for "experimental model"), this plane was Boeing's first military aircraft that came equipped with a flight deck instead of an open cockpit. From its tail to its nose, the plane measured seventy-four feet, with a wingspan of 103 feet. In addition to bombs, XB-17 came equipped with five .30-caliber machine guns mounted inside bubble windows, called "blisters."

The test results were impressive—until an Army pilot took off with the controls locked and crashed the plane.

Boeing lost the Army contract.

However, the Air Corps was so impressed that it ordered a dozen B-17s to protect America's coastlines.

In 1941, with Japan's surprise attack on Pearl Harbor, the B-17 shifted into a critical tactical weapon. It also underwent various changes, so many changes that the designers started adding sequential initials to the plane's name. The B-17 became the B-17B, then B-17C—all the way to B-17G. Some of the changes included new armor protection, self-sealing fuel tanks, super-charged engines, self-regulating oxygen systems, and gun turrets added to the plane's top, belly, and enlarged tail.

The plane's crew of nine or ten men flew at an altitude of 25,000 feet in temperatures that could drop to 30 degrees below zero! Inside the plane, ice formed on any exposed skin. Crewmen layered their bodies in wool underwear, wool socks, wool uniforms, leather jackets, leather helmets lined with sheepskin, and electric suits that heated them like electric blankets. They also wore parachutes, flak jackets, and what the troops called the "Mae West" life preserver. (Ask your parents who Mae West was). The Flying Fortress could take some serious hits and keep going. It was known to return to base with chunks of its fuselage blown off. Every time the plane went out on a mission, crews knew they might have to parachute out or crash-land.

"We lived only one day at a time..." said Glenn Simms, a B-17 gunner. "We didn't know whether we were going to live [to] tomorrow or not."

Simms flew thirty-eight missions during WWII, wedged inside the ball turret—also known as the "suicide seat." Look again at the photo at the beginning of this chapter. Would you want to be crammed inside one of those clear plastic bubbles, with enemy planes firing at you? During WWII, Simms and other B-17 gunners spent as many as 500 hours each in those blisters.

WWII waist gunners inside a B-17, wrapped up to stay warm

The final B-17G model came equipped with the following armament: twelve 50-caliber Browning M2 machine guns in the top turret; two chin guns; two belly guns; two tail guns; one waist gun left, one waist gun right; and two cheek guns.

These guns could fire 500 rounds per minute. Each gun had 150 separate parts, and every gunner was expected to know how to dismantle and replace all those parts—while blindfolded.

Why the blindfold?

Because the military knew that if the plane's instruments were damaged, these men would be firing in total darkness. At 25,000 feet altitude, the crews couldn't exactly call a repairman to come fix their guns. The gunners worked in extremely tight quarters.

Early waist gunners were stationed back-to-back, but it soon became clear this design had some problems. For one thing, the gunners kept bumping into each other. It wasn't until the G-models were developed that the waist gunner positions were staggered for maneuverability.

Another innovation for the B-17 was the Norden bombsight.

Named for its Dutch inventor who emigrated to the United States, the Norden had an analog computer that could calculate a bomb's trajectory based on current flight conditions, adjusting the path for wind, weather, and altitude. The Norden was so sensitive that when the plane approached a target, the pilot turned all controls over to the bombardier.

After releasing the bombs, the bombardier would return the controls to the pilot.

Some of the B-17's biggest problems were the windscreens that iced up—which were later changed to double-glazed windscreens—and ammunition cases so heavy they were eventually replaced by belts that fed rounds of 600 bullets to the guns.

During WWII, B-17s flew 290,000 sorties (or missions). About 4,600 planes were lost in combat, along with their crews. In 1945, at the end of WWII, the plane went out of production.

During the 1960s, some Flying Fortresses were used as target drones and destroyed by Boeing's missiles.

Today, just a few B-17s still exist.

Damaged B-17F on the ground at its base in Biskra, Algeria, Africa. The damage came from a mid-air collision with a German fighter plane over Tunisia. The B-17 made it back to base.

BOOKS

Bombing Nazi Germany: The Graphic History of the Allied Air Campaign That Defeated Hitler in World War II by Wayne Vansant

B-17 Flying Fortress in Action by David Doyle

B-17 Flying Fortress Units of the Pacific War by Martin Bowman

INTERNET

This webpage offers some good spherical depictions of the B-17. Click on the boxes such as "Under the Top Turret," and you'll get an idea of what the inside of these planes looked like: vintagetin.net/B-17Nine-O-Nine/G

WWII Database contains nearly 200 photos of the B-17, inside and out: ww2db.com/aircraft_spec.php?aircraft_model_id=a4

MOVIES

Memphis Belle

Twelve O'clock

High Air Force

THE BATTLE OF KURSK

July–August 1943

Soviet soldiers preparing their tanks for the Battle of Kursk

THE TANKS LINED up.

Thousands of tanks, stretching as far as the eye could see.

German Panzers and Tigers. Russian T-34s and T-36s.

This was the scene of the Battle of Kursk—the battle Hitler

really wanted to win.

"This offensive is of decisive importance," Hitler wrote right before the battle. "It must end in swift and decisive success. … Victory at Kursk will be a beacon for the whole world."

Why did Hitler want to win Kursk so badly?

For more than three years, Germany had been fighting unsuccessfully against the Soviet Union. With that huge loss at Stalingrad, German troop morale was at an all-time low. Even more importantly, winning Kursk would give Hitler control of that oil in the Caucasus region of Russia.

Look at the map below. You can see the town of Kursk just above the center line. The town sat just inside the Eastern Front, where German troops were fighting Stalin's Red Army.

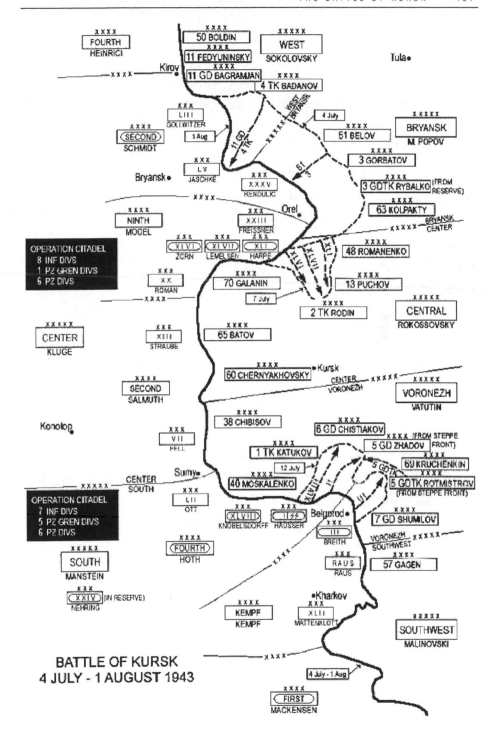

BATTLE OF KURSK
4 JULY - 1 AUGUST 1943

In the hopes of winning Kursk, Germany amassed one-third of its total military for this battle: 900,000 soldiers, 10,000 artillery guns, 2,700 tanks, and 2,000 aircraft. Hitler also ordered reconnaissance planes to photograph all the defenses being built by Stalin's military.

Stalin was well aware that this battle-to-end-all-battles was coming, thanks to British intelligence. So the Soviet dictator placed *one million* land mines across the area. He then added machine gun nests, dug-in armor, barbed wire, and anti-tank resistance points such as deep trenches that could snag a tank—anything that would make it harder for the Germans to gain mobility and cross the territory.

The Soviets planned to exhaust Hitler's forces with those defensive lines. When the Germans got tired from all that resistance, the Soviets planned to launch a massive counterattack, striking when the enemy was weak.

In this one battle, the two sides combined would unleash 2.6 million men and 7,000 tanks.

On July 5, 1943, the Germans launched their offensive. That first day, the 4th Panzer and the 9th Army saw success, but the Soviets put up such heavy resistance that the Germans immediately fell behind their planned timetable. Senior commanders began to wonder whether they had enough firepower to break through the Russian lines.

For four more days, Soviet ground troops turned the German blitzkrieg into a grinding battle. German units now knew they'd never reach Kursk in the planned time frame. Worse, the Soviets were forcing them to squander precious resources such as fuel and ammunition.

However, the German Fourth Panzer Army showed its usual dogged tenacity. Combined with smart tactics, the Panzers nearly broke the lines.

That's when the Soviets decided to counterattack.

It resulted in a monumental clash in a town called Prokho-rovka.

PROKHOROVKA

The battle within the battle

Soviet infantry of the 5th Guard Tank Army accompanies T-34/36 tanks under fire
during the Battle of Prokhorovka

In the early morning hours of July 12, German units reported hearing motors.

The Soviet tanks—hundreds of T-34s and T-36s—were speeding straight toward the stunned Germans. One Soviet tank commander described it as a "cyclone of fire unleashed by our artillery and rocket launchers."

The Germans opened fire with machine guns, armor-piercing shells, and artillery.

The Soviets jumped from their tanks, took cover, and left

the armored vehicles to roll forward. The Germans eventually destroyed them but the Soviet bombardment was turning the battlefield into a swirling chaos of black smoke and dust and screams. Soviet soldiers shouted, "Sta! Sta! Sta!" (or "Steel! Steel! Steel!")—the code word to release more tanks.

As the enormous cloud of smoke and dust headed their way, the Germans dispatched warnings to the other tank unit. But the Panzer commanders weren't trained to improvise in battle. They were taught to follow a precise routine for every attack: stop the tank, identify the enemy target, let the tank's gunner line up the victim in his sights, and *then* give the order to open fire. This routine was rehearsed so often that the process took only seconds inside the tank.

The sudden onslaught of Soviet tanks left the Panzer crews no time between firings. "Suddenly a T-34 broke through and headed right for us," recalled German tank crewman Wilhelm Res. "Our first radio operator started giving me shells to put into the gun. At this time, our commander above us was shouting 'Fire! Fire!' nonstop, because the tank was getting closer; and only after the fourth 'Fire!' I heard 'Thank God!'"

Heavy black smoke choked the Kursk battlefield. Tanks whirled. Guns fired. Land mines exploded. Commanders on both sides struggled to identify their own forces.

Despite the German's rigid style, the experienced Panzer crews excelled in such difficult circumstances. The German tanks also had radios, so they could communicate with each other and their commanders. Clever tactics combined with clear thinking helped the German forces destroy more Soviet tanks than they lost themselves. Overhead, the Luftwaffe inflicted still more damage on Stalin's force.

Soviet tank regiments took on suicide runs, firing their

76mm guns on the Germans even though nothing could pierce the armor of the German Tiger. One entire Soviet regiment was annihilated this way, leaving in its wake burning tanks that smoldered into the night.

Fighting against this offensive, the Germans were able to push the Soviets back to where they'd started earlier that day.

So Germany could claim a tactical victory, but in reality, neither side accomplished what it set out to do. The battle at Prokhorovka was more like a draw, and it created even bigger problems for Germany. For the first time, its army was stopped before it could break enemy lines, and the Soviets still outnumbered the Germans in armored vehicles almost two to one—about 300 tanks for Germany versus the Soviet's 600-plus. The Soviet air force also battered the Luftwaffe so badly that the Germans struggled to keep an operational air fleet.

And yet, the Germans didn't retreat. For several days, the fighting persisted.

On July 16, the 3rd Panzer Corps linked up with another division and encircled several Soviet rifle divisions. They also gained several hills, giving them a tactical advantage. Field commanders begged Hitler to keep fighting. Historians believe that Germany could've won the Battle of Kursk, and WWII would've turned out differently.

Whether it was that great loss at Stalingrad or some sudden attack of nerves—or the news that the Allies had just invaded Sicily—Hitler suddenly recalled his troops from Kursk.

The battle convinced Hitler that his military leaders were incompetent. After Kursk, he started making even more military command decisions.

By the end of August, Russia had won the Battle of Kursk.

Yet, despite the victory, Russia lost more than three times as many troops as the Germans—about 175,000 men—and more than 1,600 armored vehicles and 460 aircraft.

Germany lost 252 tanks and 159 aircraft.

The battle also inflicted about 200,000 casualties on the civilians living in Kursk.

While Hitler intervened more frequently in his military's battles after Kursk, Stalin did the exact opposite. The Soviet dictator stepped back from command and gave more power to his military commanders.

WHO FOUGHT?

German Tiger I, steamrolling across France in 1944

What does the German word "panzer" mean? It's actually a shortened term for the word *panzerkampfwagen*, which translates as "armored fighting vehicle."

So basically, "panzer" means "armor." In Hitler's army, it stood for the tank divisions.

Ironically, Germany's most heavily-armored tank wasn't a Panzer at all. It was the Tiger.

In addition to light- and medium-weight tanks, Germany developed this heavy tank. The Tiger sent shivers down an enemy's spine. Weighing more than sixty tons, it carried a 88mm gun and was so heavily armored it could survive hits from infantry, anti-tank devices, and other tanks.

During the North Africa campaign, the Allied forces were so intimidated by the Tiger's strengths that British General Bernard Montgomery banned any talk about it.

But the Tiger wasn't perfect.

This enormous beast had to be maintained. Not only was it built from expensive materials, the Tiger guzzled fuel, giving it a limited range. The Tiger's weight and size also made it difficult to transport, and when it broke down, several vehicles were needed to tow it. In fact, the Tiger was so heavy that it crushed road pavement.

Meanwhile, the Soviets had the T-34 tank. It was built for speed, bad weather, and rough terrain. With its sloped armor, it also deflected shells better. The T-34's agility bedeviled the Germans.

So the Germans developed the Panzer V tank. It had a large turret, a 75mm gun, and a powerful engine. But Germany rushed its production, causing most of those Panzers to later break down from mechanical failures.

In 1944, Germany perfected the Panzer. It also developed the Tiger II, a version that cut back operational costs. The Allies had nothing that could match these tanks.

Fortunately, by 1944, the Allies were bombing German factories and severely crippling Hitler's ability to churn out these devastating monsters of the battlefield.

BOOKS

KURSK: The Greatest Tank Battle by M.K. Barbier

Kursk 1943: The Northern Front by Robert Forczyk

INTERNET

Look inside a German Tiger 1 Tank:
   youtube.com/watch?v=xFzlZbfpQUo

Find out more about each type of tank involved in the Battle of Kursk: www.battleofkursk.org/Battle-of-Kursk-Tanks.html

MOVIES

World War II Episode 15 Kursk Battle (2006)

The Russian Front: From Stalingrad to Kursk (DVD)

THE BATTLE OF SALERNO

OPERATION AVALANCHE
September 3–16, 1943

German soldiers fire a Pak 40 gun near Salerno, Italy, late September 1943

WHEN THE NEWS came over the speakers, General Mark Clark was aboard a transport ship, finishing dinner with his men of the Fifth Army.

What was the news?

Italy had surrendered, and the Germans didn't know it.

Clark and his men cheered. The Fifth Army was at that moment heading for Italy as part of the Allied invasion force of the mainland. Now that Italy was on the Allies' side, Clark figured the invasion would take only about three days.

Unfortunately, Clark was dead wrong.

Not only were the Germans still waiting for the Allies, they knew all about Italy's "secret" surrender. On September 9, before dawn, the first men in the invasion quietly climbed down the transport ship's cargo nets and settled into the landing craft. Armed for the fight, packed tight as sardines, they were part of the Navy's 4th Beach Battalion. Known as "knee deepers," these guys were predecessors to today's Navy SEALs, trained to fight under the most challenging circumstances on both land and water.

"You can say we were the forerunners of groups like the SEALS," said Al Benevelli, one of WWII's Knee Deepers, "except without [their] equipment. We had a gun, a pack, some TNT, and our life belt. There was no distinctive uniform in those times. We wore dungarees."

The Knee Deepers' job was to smooth the transition for other troops from ship to shore. They cleared sights for the landing craft, unloaded equipment, removed obstacles such as barbed wire, and repaired anything damaged in the landing—usually while under fire and still communicating back to the ships. They were also in charge of evacuating casualties.

Code named Operation Avalanche, this invasion called for British, American, and Canadian troops to land at two separate beaches. One force would land near the "heel" of Italy. Another at Salerno, higher, in southwest Italy (see map). These forces would then travel up the Italian coast toward Naples where a small contingent of American Rangers and British Commandos would land, securing the roads that led into Naples.

The British and Canadian troops hit the heel of Italy with no opposition.

But Clark's Fifth Army wasn't so fortunate. In fact, the landing at Salerno turned into one of the worst military blunders of WWII.

The Allies were hoping to use the element of surprise by invading around 3:30 a.m. so there wouldn't be any pre-invasion naval bombardment.

But Germany already planned for the invasion, and was ready to hit back with as much force as possible. Hitler had sent in reinforcements, removed Rommel, and replaced him with General Albert Kesselring, who wasted no time salting the Salerno beachhead with land mines and positioning 88mm guns to inflict enormous damage on the arriving Allies.

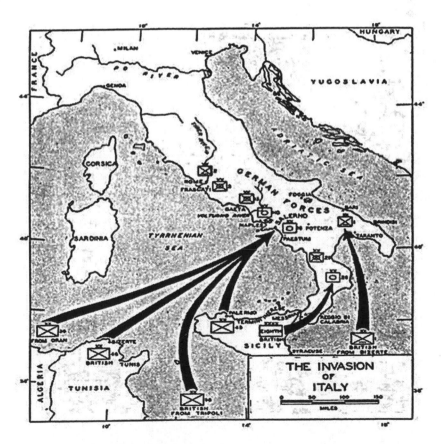

In the dark of night, as the men of the Fifth moved across the sand, the Luftwaffe suddenly swooped overhead, strafing bullets across the beach. German Tiger tanks rolled forward, blasting fire from their huge guns. The only thing that kept the tanks from flattening the soldiers were the Germans' own land mines.

The "easy" landing turned into a deadly mess. Americans tried to radio the naval ships for fire support, but the radios weren't working or they'd been dropped on the beach during the surprise attack. Finally, some radio operators managed to dispatch a message for help. But the ships' firepower wound up killing Allied troops because the vessels didn't know where the landing forces were on the beach.

In the midst of all that gunfire from both sides, one navy signalman tied together some white handkerchiefs and stood up. He waved them, sending a signal code message to the Allied ships, and redirected their fire to the German tanks. That one brave man changed the course of this first day.

By the afternoon, Allied reinforcements made it to shore.

The three-day schedule General Clark boasted about stretched into twenty-one days of bloody fighting and death. Years later, the landing at Salerno would divide historians. Some considered Clark an incompetent glory-hound who unnecessarily got Americans killed; others insisted most of the Mediterranean battles were difficult, even for seasoned leaders, and this invasion was Clark's first time as field commander. Patton had been "exiled" and forced to stay in Sicily after slapping some enlisted men and calling them cowards (yes, really).

The Allied plan had another crucial problem. It depended on Germany concentrating its forces in northern Italy. The

Allies thought Hitler would leave the southern terrain unde-
fended. However, when Kesselring replaced Rommel,
Germany changed its defensive plan. Kesselring hunkered
down with his forces in southern Italy's steep mountains,
placing his troops in the best position for maximum slaughter.

The Allies had to fight for every inch of "surrendered" Italy.

About a week later, British General Montgomery's forces
had almost reached Salerno. Kesselring, realizing the Allies
might join forces, ordered his troops to fall back and form a
defensive line. Even if the Allies managed to take Salerno,
Kesselring believed the mountainous terrain would favor his
defenses. The Germans had also destroyed the area's bridges
and roads, further slowing the Allied advance.

British troops advance around a burning German Panzer tank, near Salerno, Italy

Kesselring's forces only gave up ground at the slowest possible rate. Whenever the Germans pulled back, the British troops, along with the American Fifth, only pushed forward harder.

By late September, the Allies had secured control of southern Italy. But the German defensive lines stretched across Italy, blocking access to the North. The Nazis hoped to buy time and build an even stronger defensive line further north, near Rome. In the meantime, they inflicted casualties among the Allies. These Germans—and the Italians who still supported them— were skilled fighters who used the hills and serpentine roads to ruin any Allied movement of mechanized equipment. The Allied air attacks also struggled against the steep mountains.

Then, on September 14, more than 500 B-25s, B-26s, and B-17s—that Flying Fortress—struck the German forces. Allied ships backed up the bombers—with one ship alone firing one thousand 6-inch rounds. For all that, the Allies gained only two hundred yards of beach.

And lost many men.

Kesselring planned to shove the Allies off the beach, but he failed.

The Allies planned to come ashore and race up north to fight the Germans there, but they failed.

Instead, it would take the Allies nineteen months to move into northern Italy. The slow movement added heavy losses of life, fighting one German defensive line after another.

During the first week of Salerno alone, more than 2,000 Allied troops were killed and another 7,050 were wounded. More than 3,000 were missing or captured.

All that time, General Clark stayed in the front lines during the battle, leading his men. He was later awarded the Distinguished Service Cross.

WHO FOUGHT?

Some Italian Resistance fighters in Naples

Many ordinary citizens helped the Allies liberate Italy.

Some were guerrilla fighters, working with the secret Resistance opposing Mussolini and the Nazi occupation. The guerrillas hid in abandoned barns and caves. Working in small groups, they used their familiarity with the local terrain to ambush German soldiers. They also snuck onto farms at night and borrowed large animals to move equipment, returning the animals by morning.

In the cities, the Italian Resistance developed a network of safe houses used to hide weapons, supplies, and take care of wounded fighters.

The occupying Germans, realizing how loyal the Italian people were to these guerrilla fighters, started inflicting harsh punishments. For instance, if an Italian killed a German soldier, the Nazis would kill ten Italians in retribution.

However, these cruel punishments backfired. The Italians

only felt more loyalty toward the Resistance. As the war continued, more Italians grew to dislike their dictator, Benito Mussolini. Finally, in April 1943, Mussolini and his girlfriend were executed by the Italian people and hung upside down as a sign of complete disrespect.

When Italy surrendered to the Allies in September 1943, the Italian people felt further emboldened against the Nazis.

More than 200 Italians helped three companies of American soldiers with the 88th Infantry Division attack a hill occupied by the German 290th Grenadier Regiment. Not only did the Allies capture the hill, they held it for five days against German reinforcements. These kinds of victories helped clear a path for the Allied forces advancing north from Salerno.

But the most famous fight among Italian citizens took place in the city of Naples.

During WWII, Naples suffered through 105 bombings that killed more than 25,000 people and wounded tens of thousands more.

In late September 1943, as Allied troops pushed north from Salerno, the people of Naples took hold of any weapon available—from kitchen knives to broom handles. Children jumped into the Gulf of Napoli and retrieved any guns that were dumped there. Furniture—even toilets—were tossed from balconies into the roads to block German tanks from getting around town.

The riot in Naples lasted four days.

On October 1, as Allied forces marched into Naples expecting a firefight, they found the city completely cleared of German forces.

For their actions during WWII, the people of Naples were awarded a Gold Medal of Military Valor.

BOOKS

Salerno 1943: The Allies invade southern Italy by Angus Konstam and Steve Noon

P-38 Lightning Aces of the 82nd Fighter Group by Steve Blake and Chris Davey

Omar Bradley by Steven J. Zaloga

The Liberator: One World War II Soldier's 500-Day Odyssey from the Beaches of Sicily to the Gates of Dachau by Alex Kershaw

INTERNET

YouTube video with excellent historic footage of Operation Avalanche, The Battle of Salerno: youtube.com/watch?v=5O8b5mM6Zdc

More about the Four Days of Naples: www.napoliunplugged.com/the-four-days-of-naples-september-27-october-1-1943-le-quattro-giornate-di-napoli.html

Want to read more about WWII in general? Check out this website for a WWII magazine: www.historynet.com/world-war-ii

MOVIES

The Four Days of Naples dramatizes the citizen uprising that cleared the town of German occupiers. It was nominated for two Academy Awards.

D-DAY: OPERATION OVERLORD

June 6, 1944

American soldiers crouch for cover as invasion forces sail for the Normandy beaches, June 6, 1944

YOU JUST HEARD about the disaster created by the invasion of Salerno. And you remember Operation Mincemeat, when British spies played a great trick on Hitler, which probably saved the invasion of Sicily.

The Allies next planned to invade occupied France. They would be knocking on Hitler's door.

For the invasion to succeed, the Allies needed to come up with more clever tricks. For four years, German forces had been in France, growing familiar with the roads and the terrain. They'd also built up massive defenses, including enormous cannons that faced the coastal waters, and they were led by the formidable General Rommel and his ferocious fighters.

For this invasion, later known as D-Day, the Allies' trick didn't rely on a dead body.

Instead, they used the very much alive General George Patton.

Patton was known for his fierce fighting style both on and off the battlefield. Patton shared some common military traits with the Germans—fast, aggressive attacks and merciless fighting—which earned the respect of Germany's military leaders. Because Patton also won most of his battles, the Nazis assumed the Allies would put him in charge of any invasion of France.

So the Germans decided to shadow Patton. They thought that Patton's movements would reveal the Allies' next step.

Since the Allies knew the Germans were watching Patton, the general became the bait on their hook.

The Allies gave Patton a fake army, called the First US Army Group. It included troops and armaments. But in reality, the tanks were actually giant balloons! From a distance, these balloons looked just like real armored vehicles. Patton also commanded an entire fleet of airplanes—that had wooden propellers incapable of getting the planes off the ground. Finally, the Allies stationed Patton's "force" in Dover, England where German reconnaissance planes would fly over, checking out this "base." Patton's troops would fire on the recon planes—but only enough to seem mad. They actually wanted the Germans to see everything.

Meanwhile, throughout Britain, under the utmost secrecy, the Allies were training the invasion's real ground, air, and naval forces.

In the spring of 1944, knowing the Nazis were shadowing him, Patton walked into an English pub. The general pretended to drink too much alcohol, then acted really drunk. Later, as he staggered out the door, Patton called out to some Allied soldiers in the pub, "Hey! I guess I'll see you in Calais!"

Calais is a French port located on the English Channel, at the narrowest point between England and France. For a long time, Germany had suspected the Allies would use Calais for a French invasion because of the short water crossing and because Calais had a harbor.

Now Patton's drunken words confirmed the Germans' suspicions.

These strategies—and many others—were part of the elaborate net of diversion needed for the D-Day invasion. The Allies knew that a successful invasion of France would shift the war and put Hitler on the defensive. He would see the Allies were coming for him. However, if this invasion failed, it would cost thousands of lives—civilian and military—giving Hitler a significant advantage.

"Full victory—nothing less," said General Eisenhower, Supreme Commander of the Allied Forces.

General Eisenhower, addressing American paratroopers right before they would jump into France on D-Day

To fool the Germans even further, the Allies developed a bunch of other invasion plans. Operation Fortitude, for instance, showed the Allies invading Norway. Operation Bodyguard and Zeppelin outlined the invasion of Greece. Operation Anvil was an invasion of Spain. Operation Vendetta explained how to invade through the Mediterranean.

All of these operations were fake.

The real invasion was Operation Overlord where troops would land at Normandy, France.

Look at the map. Normandy is a region in northern France. Also, see Calais further to the east, directly across from Dover, England—where Patton was leading his "troops."

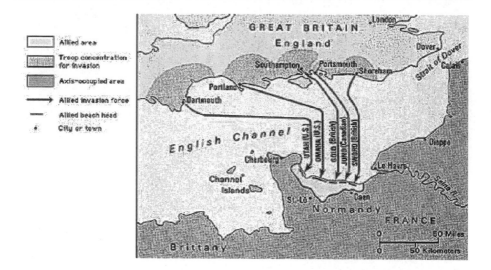

"D-Day" is a military term. It means "the day an attack will begin."

For Normandy, the D-Day invasion was carefully chosen by Allied military planners. They factored in everything from convoy transport times, weather, tides, phases of the moon, and the beaches. They chose June 5, 1944.

But on June 4, the weather suddenly turned. The sky was heavily overcast—risking aerial plans—and strong winds blew across the raging ocean. Huge waves crashed on the beaches.

These were terrible conditions for an invasion.

However, the just-right conditions weren't expected for at least another week. By then, Germany would probably figure out the Allies' plan and attack. D-Day would be another disaster.

So, despite the bad conditions, General Eisenhower ordered the invasion to begin. Eisenhower's exact words?

"O.K., let's go."

That might sound like a casual way to launch WWII's biggest invasion, but nothing could be further from the truth. As leader of the Allied forces, Eisenhower knew how risky this mission was. The Nazis had more than fifty divisions in France, led by Rommel, who had placed thousands of armed fortifications along the Normandy beaches. Eisenhower sent a pre-invasion letter to every Allied soldier, sailor, and pilot, encouraging them to face this tough battle with bravery and confidence in their abilities.

But Eisenhower also drafted another letter, in case of failure. It read:

"Our landings in the Cherbourg-Havre area [Normandy] have failed to gain a satisfactory foothold and I have withdrawn the troops. My decision to attack at this time and place was based upon the best information available. The troops, the air, and the Navy did all that bravery and devotion to duty could do. If any blame or fault attaches to the attempt it is mine alone."

Eisenhower put that letter aside, and waited for the invasion to begin.

Just after midnight, as June 5 turned into June 6, Allied planes flew in the dark over Normandy carrying the Pathfinders. These men were a special group of paratroopers, trained to prevent some of the mistakes that had occurred in other invasions. Since pilots sometimes struggled to locate their exact drops, especially at night, the Pathfinders were going in first to place transponders on the ground. These boxes would send signals to the planes, directing the pilots to the drop zone.

But this phase of the invasion didn't go as planned.

Seeing the planes, the Germans opened fire. The anti-aircraft flak was so heavy that pilots decided to fly higher and faster than normal. As the 20,000 American, British, and Canadian paratroopers leapt into the dark, stiff winds blew them off course. Paratroopers missed their landings by as much as twenty miles, placing them deep in enemy territory.

A wave of the paratroopers drop into Normandy on June 6, 1944

Fortunately the paratroopers had a trick—dummy jumpers.

Shaped like real men, these dummies were wired with ammunition. When they hit the ground, the dummies fired "guns." Not only did these dummies surprise the enemy, they made the Germans think there were far more paratroopers than there actually were. With the wind scattering the airborne troops, the German couldn't locate the invasion's exact position.

As soon as they landed, the paratroopers started securing the area's bridges and crossroads. Glider pilots also slipped over the terrain, helping to secure more structures.

Meanwhile, on the north Atlantic Ocean, an Allied armada covered the water:

5,000 ships

1,400 troops transport vessels

805 cargo vessels

138 war ships

221 escort vessels

"This vast operation," Churchill said of D-Day, "is un-
doubtedly the most complicated and difficult that has ever
occurred."

Landing craft and Allied troops in Normandy, France, D-Day 1944. Notice the
barrage balloons in the air above the beach. These explosive balloons protected the
Allies from low-flying enemy aircraft.

The D-Day invasion centered on five beaches. Each beach
was given a code name. The American troops would land on
Utah and Omaha Beaches. British forces would land on Gold
and Sword. The Canadians would take Juno.

Unlike Calais, Normandy had no harbors for unloading supplies and staging an attack. To remedy that situation, British engineers designed Mulberry harbors and Phoenix breakwaters. These structures were gigantic concrete blocks, dumped into the water, that created an immediate port and breakers to calm the ocean waves.

Utah Beach was the most successful landing. Approximately 1,800 vehicles and 21,000 troops reached the beach, suffering only a few hundred casualties. Later, Utah would be called the smoothest amphibious landing in American history.

The Canadians landing at Juno Beach had the farthest objective, compared to the other landings. Also, the Germans had excellent defensive positions above that beach. Yet 21,400 men made it ashore, with about 1,200 casualties.

At Sword Beach, 25,000 British troops landed, suffering only 400 casualties. The 6th Airborne took good positions and were able to neutralize Germany's large coastal guns.

So it looked like all that secrecy surrounding the Normandy invasion had paid off. The German troops were caught totally off guard. For instance, the Luftwaffe only had two planes— two!—and Rommel wasn't anywhere near the invasion. He had gone to Paris to buy shoes for his wife's birthday.

And Hitler?

Hitler was asleep when the D-Day invasion began. When his men received the news, they were afraid to wake him up— Hitler had a bad temper. But even after Hitler finally heard the news about D-Day, he thought it was a diversion. He was certain the real invasion would be at Calais with Patton. So Hitler held back Germany's reserve tank division.

Just one of Germany's many coastal guns aimed at the Atlantic Ocean. Look closely at the sign below the gun's barrel. The battery was named "Lundemann," in honor of the captain of the sunken Bismarck.

However, D-Day wasn't a smooth operation. Two of the beach landings were slaughters.

The Germans had 8,000 permanent bunkers around Normandy, including machine gun nests and artillery, with another 2,300 anti-tank guns, 2,700 guns that were greater than 75mm, and *four million* exploding mines.

When Britain's 1st New Hampshire regiment hit Gold Beach, the Germans wiped them out, killing or wounding an entire regiment.

The Americans on Omaha Beach had it even worse.

Germany had positioned hundreds of machine gun nests above this four-mile stretch of sand. When the first wave of Americans headed toward shore, those guns opened fire. The Americans were crossing in specially designed Higgins boats whose front walls dropped and turned into ramps. But sitting inside these boats, the American men were positioned like fish in a barrel.

So many men were getting killed inside these landing craft that soldiers demanded to get out immediately, right there, in the water. The Higgins boats dropped their ramps, but they were about five football fields away from the beach. The soldiers wore life preservers, but the equipment inside their packs weighed more than sixty pounds and pulled men underwater, drowning them in the cold Atlantic.

Those that survived the water waded to shore through zinging gunfire. If they reached the sand, land mines exploded.

Then, they found "Rommel's asparagus." The German general had designed special angled spikes with mines attached to the ends. When the spikes were touched, they exploded.

The first wave on Omaha Beach. Tanks are sinking. "Rommel's asparagus" mines stick out of the water. The beach held still more exploding mines, and German gun nests fire from the cliffs.

Half of the men in that first wave of soldiers at Omaha were killed.

Twenty-nine tanks were also sent out. All but two sank.

Howitzers were lost as well. On the beach, the Americans were left defending themselves with whatever weapons they carried—pistols, rifles—shooting against German machine guns.

So many engineers were killed in the first wave that the Omaha beach hadn't been cleared of mines and other deadly obstacles.

The invasion looked like an utter failure.

From the ships, military leaders watched the slaughter on Omaha. Naval commanders pushed their destroyers to within one thousand yards of the beach. It was a really risky move. Ships that size require a significant amount of water under their hulls or else they'll get grounded. The destroyers managed to fire on the German nests, helping the men on the beach.

Major General Norman Cota was among the highest ranking officers on Omaha Beach. Cota realized that even with the slaughter, this mission would have to continue. This beach was close to many roads and intersections. Having control of the area would allow the Allies to mobilize more troops. Amid the smoke and fire and death, Cota organized the troops. Soon the Army Rangers showed up. Cota hollered, "If you are Rangers, lead the way!"

Ever since, the Rangers' motto has been "Rangers lead the way."

But for every single yard of beach gained at Omaha, one American soldier was killed. There were 2,400 casualties on that first day.

Over the next six days, however, the five beach invasions

managed to link forces. Airborne support helped the ground forces to push inland. Eight more divisions came ashore—a total of 326,000 Allied troops—and more than 50,000 vehicles.

In the Normandy invasion, the Allies suffered more than 11,000 casualties. More than 4,000 men were dead.

The Germans suffered more than 200,000 casualties—killed, wounded, or captured—in part because they didn't realize Normandy was the real location for the invasion. By the time they figured out Calais was a trick, the Allies already had a toehold in France.

With help from the guerrilla fighters in the French Resistance, the Allies began knocking out railroads. They cut electricity and underground telephone cables. For the rest of June and into July, the Allies pushed forward through German firefights.

Paris, the capital of France, had been under German rule since its surrender in 1940. But on August 19, Resistance fighters attacked a German garrison near Paris. This action was the beginning of the end. One week later, the Germans surrendered Paris.

Historian Stephen Ambrose interviewed many of the men involved in the D-Day invasion. He wrote about one Allied lieutenant who later that day was "walking around among the sleeping men and thinking to himself that they had looked at and smelled death all around them all day but never even dreamed of applying the term to themselves. They hadn't come here to fear. They hadn't come to die. They had come to win."

WHO FOUGHT?

US soldiers helping troops from their sinking landing craft on Omaha Beach,
June 6, 1944

In 1944, the tiny town of Bedford, Virginia had only about 3,000 residents.

But thirty-five of its young men were serving in armed forces during WWII. Most of these men were in Company A of the 116th Infantry. That company was part of the first wave to hit Omaha Beach. Nineteen Bedford men died in that landing. Six of them drowned. Four more died in later D-Day battles.

Ray Nance was among the Bedford soldiers in the first wave on Omaha Beach. He later described what it was like riding in the landing craft toward shore.

"The minute the ramp went down [the Germans] opened up. We must have been torn up pretty badly. A good many men were killed on the ramp."

With water up to his chest, Nance waded toward shore. All around him, men were dying. Only three soldiers on Nance's boat weren't killed or injured. When Nance made it to the beach, his situation only grew worse.

"A bullet passed through my pack and clothing, cutting the strap on my binocular case. We were caught in very heavy machine gun fire."

The next bullets struck him in the stomach and foot.

Nance lived, but the twenty-three Bedford soldiers who died in D-Day were later known as "The Bedford Boys."

Years later, when the United States Congress was searching for a location to build a D-Day Memorial to honor the sacrifices at Normandy, it chose the otherwise obscure mountain town of Bedford, Virginia.

You can visit the D-Day Memorial online: www.dday.org

Be sure to listen to stories from D-Day veterans: www.dday.org/education-quick-links-95/stories-from-veterans

BOOKS

Our Finest Day: D-Day, June 6, 1944 by Mark Bowden and Stephen E. Ambrose

Overlord: D-Day and the Battle for Normandy by Max Hastings

LIFE D-Day: Remembering the Battle that Won the War – 70 Years Later by the editors of *LIFE*

D-Day (Young Reading Series 3) by Henry Brook

Steck-Vaughn Timeline Graphic Novels: D-Day

The Pointblank Directive: Three Generals and the Untold Story of the Daring Plan that Saved D-Day by L. Keeney

The Bedford Boys: One American Town's Ultimate D-day Sacrifice by Alex Kershaw

The quote from Stephen Ambrose comes from his larger study of D-Day: *Band of Brothers: E Company, 506th Regiment, 101st Airborne*

INTERNET

Excellent slide show of the D-Day planning and invasion. Use your cursor to zoom into the images for close-ups: google.com/culturalinstitute/exhibit/d-day-and-the-normandy-invasion/wRQ7nqwa

WWII newsreel cameraman Jack Lieb used his personal footage to recount the movements from the D-Day preparations in England to the liberation of Paris, and later Germany. Lieb narrates the tour, in which you will see some celebrities at war, such as actor Edward G. Robinson and writer Ernest Hemingway. unwritten-record.blogs.archives.gov/2014/06/05/a-newsreel-cameramans-view-of-d-day

Visit the D-Day Memorial Museum online: www.dday.org

MOVIES

The Longest Day

Where Eagles Dare

Eye of the Needle

Saving Private Ryan: Its 27-minute opening sequence offers an authentic recreation of the landing at Omaha (Caution: violence and language)

BATTLE OF THE BULGE

December 16, 1944–January 28, 1945

American soldiers in defensive positions in the Ardennes, December 1944

HITLER WAS IN trouble.

Italy was lost.

Paris was liberated.

And Stalin had blocked Germany's attacks on the Eastern Front.

Now Stalin's forces were marching west toward Germany while the Allies were shifting troops into Belgium, right next door to Germany.

Soon, Hitler would be surrounded.

He needed a major victory, right away.

Back in the beginning of WWII, one of Germany's most decisive victories took place in Belgium. The Nazis conquered the tiny northern European country in just two weeks.

In late 1944, Hitler decided to return to the scene of the crime. He would attack Belgium once again.

It was a shrewd strategic idea.

Allied forces were stretched from southern Italy all the way to the Netherlands. Those long distances created problems for supply lines. Militarily, some areas were stronger than others. The Allies' weakest link was probably Belgium. The American troops stationed there were mostly novice fighters who had never seen combat.

Hitler was also shrewd about striking in the dead of winter. Belgium's notoriously overcast skies and icy fogs would keep Allied aircraft grounded.

Hitler's goal was to recapture the Belgian seaport of Antwerp. It sits on the English Channel, right across from Britain. From there, Hitler planned to force Great Britain and the United States to negotiate for peace. With the Allies out of the war picture, Hitler could unleash his full military force against the Soviets, finally winning the Eastern Front.

Although the Allies suspected Hitler would strike at some point, they didn't know when or where. Unfortunately, after winning Italy and parts of France, the Allies were feeling complacent—satisfied with how things were going. It looked like Germany was losing the war.

But Hitler was already assembling his forces to strike Belgium: 300,000 men, 1,900 artillery pieces, and 1,000 tanks and armored vehicles.

You would expect the Allies to notice such a massive buildup. But they didn't. Hitler executed his plan with great cunning. He suspected the Allies had broken the German code, so he didn't dispatch orders over the radio. Instead, he sent dispatches by motorcycle couriers. He also moved the military equipment and troops at night under cover of darkness.

The Allies never saw Hitler coming into Belgium.

But they would never forget what happened next.

The Battle of the Bulge would be the costliest action ever fought by the US Army. When it was over, America alone would suffer some 100,000 casualties.

Heavily armed German soldier in the Ardennes Offensive, December 1944

In the cold dark hours before dawn on December 16, Germany attacked.

The 6th Panzer division's artillery barrage stretched across eighty miles. They hit command posts, troop encampments, and communication centers. Ninety minutes later, German foot soldiers marched out from the icy fog, shooting to kill.

With so many of the American soldiers never having seen combat, the German's sudden devastating tank and artillery attack scared them into breaking and running. Yet enough Americans stayed to fire back and hold off a total rout.

In the initial attack's northern section, a single American reconnaissance platoon and four Forward Artillery Observers dug into a ridge overlooking a key road intersection. These men managed to delay the 6th Panzer Army for almost 24 hours.

In the thickly forested Ardennes region, heavy snowstorms blanketed the ground. The snow had grounded Allied planes but it also created obstacles for Allied tanks, which were slowed even further by poor communications.

Roads offered strategic superiority, so Germany's 5th Panzer Army headed to the town of Bastogne, while the 7th Panzer Army pushed toward the country of Luxembourg to the south (see map). The plan was to flank the Allies.

But the American 99th Infantry Division held its ground in the north—even after losing 2,000 men in a single day. When the 2nd Division slipped through enemy lines, the combined American forces formed an unbreakable barrier. Infantry from Germany's 6th Panzers continued to attack, but these "novice" fighters put up a surprising amount of resistance.

Although outnumbered five to one, the 99th soldiers inflicted casualties on the Germans with a ratio of eighteen to one.

Historians later said these men of the 2nd and 99th Divisions, fighting as underdogs in Belgium's freezing weather, changed the entire campaign in the Ardennes.

Another reconnaissance platoon of eighteen Americans delayed a German battalion of 500, holding them back for ten hours. The Americans inflicted ninety-two casualties.

All this resistance ruined the schedule set by the Germans.

The next day, Hitler's forces fired back with a vengeance. They captured parts of the 3rd Battalion of the 394th Infantry Regiment and took control of an American fuel depot. After gassing up their tanks, the Germans rolled westward.

To the north, Panzer divisions were capturing crucial roads.

German troops fighting in the Ardennes. The soldier in the foreground is equipped with a StG-44, the world's first assault rifle.

For more than a week, the Americans kept up their stiff resistance. However, by Christmas, the Germans had captured more roads and villages. Soon they would reach Antwerp—possibly even France.

General Eisenhower grew concerned.

"I didn't get frightened until three weeks after it had begun," Eisenhower later said of the Battle of the Bulge, "when I began to read the American papers and found... how near we were to being whipped."

The Allies needed a fast, decisive counterattack. Otherwise Hitler would win this battle.

Eisenhower dispatched 250,000 soldiers, along with thousands of tanks. He also imposed a news blackout. The American public wouldn't hear about the largest ground battle on WWII's western front for several days. Not coincidentally, Hitler wanted the news to get out—he thought this deadly battle would change the American public's sentiments about the war and convince the Allies to surrender to Germany. As troops and armor poured in from all sides of Belgium, Eisenhower's counterplan was to squeeze together the Panzer columns, choking the German advance and keeping them from reaching Antwerp or France.

That's how this battle got its name—the counterattack on the German advance created a "bulge" in the front line.

But the Germans were determined to win, and they believed the Allied counterattack would spill even more blood on the Belgian snow.

THE MALMEDY MASSACRE

The aftermath of the Malmedy Massacre, American soldiers dead on the ground

On a snowy field near Malmedy, Belgium, German troops captured 130 American soldiers who were part of the 285th Field Artillery Observation Battalion. Lining up the Americans, the Germans proceeded to take all their possessions—wallets, rings, and cigarettes.

Then the German troop leader commanded: "Kill them all."

The Germans opened fire. Seventy American soldiers were killed. The others, running in every direction, escaped.

Later, these killings were called the Malmedy Massacre.

American troops in Belgium during the Battle of the Bulge

In other parts of the country, the Allied troops were suffering the ravages of cold weather, compounded by the fact that some of them didn't have even the most basic winter clothing such as gloves. There also wasn't enough medicine to treat the wounded, and ammunition supplies were running low.

Meanwhile, the Germans were going all out for this battle. Infiltrating Allied lines with German soldiers who spoke English, Hitler's men captured American jeeps then strapped on US Military Police armbands. Standing at key road junctions, these fake MPs gave false directions to Allied forces. They also turned signposts so the markers pointed the wrong way. Red ribbons on the roads were supposed to mark where the land mines were located, but these infiltrators moved them, leading the Allies right into the land mines.

These tricks confused the already dazed Americans. When word spread about these tricks and the Malmedy executions, American soldiers became determined to make Germany pay. They combined infantry units and made good use of hand grenades and their M-1 rifles. The battle turned even fiercer, often raging toward the goal of gaining one foot of ground, over and over again.

When temperatures dropped down to zero, American troops stuffed newspapers into their clothing and boots for insulation. Other men took drapes from abandoned farmhouses and used them as rags to wrap their feet. Frostbite, trench foot, and pneumonia became common. The c-rations of food turned into blocks of ice. Water froze inside canteens. When soldiers finally managed to fall asleep, they woke up encased in ice.

BASTOGNE

M4 Sherman tank and troops from Company G, 740th Tank Battalion, 504th Regiment, and US 82nd Airborne Division, struggle through the bitter winter in Belgium, January, 1945

For the Germans, the town of Bastogne was a key junction point. The town had five main roads and two secondary roads, all of which would help move mechanized forces toward their main objective—the port of Antwerp.

Realizing Bastogne's importance, Eisenhower sent the 101st Airborne Division there, led by Brigadier General Anthony McAuliffe. As the reinforcements came in, American troops were fleeing deadly German attacks. McAuliffe organized the remaining troops, set up a defense of Bastogne, and ordered the various units—about 18,000 men—to hold a sixteen-mile perimeter.

The deadly fighting continued.

Six days later, the Germans sent McAuliffe an ultimatum—surrender or get slaughtered.

McAuliffe replied to their demand with one word: "Nuts."

Translation: No way.

Eisenhower had also sent General Patton's Third Army to Belgium. The controversial general put his men into overdrive.

"This time," Patton said, "the German stuck his hand in a meat grinder and I've got the handle."

Patton's Third Army would move faster and engage more enemy divisions than any other army in American history.

Finally, on December 23, the skies over Belgium literally cleared.

Allied air forces flew into action, striking the enemy from above while hundreds of C-47 cargo planes dropped desperately needed supplies.

With Patton's army pounding the German lines, a sense of hope rippled through the Bastogne forces. But on Christmas morning, the Germans delivered another brutal attack. So brutal that many American soldiers shook hands and said goodbye. The fighting was so fierce that army cooks, clerks, and mechanics joined the fight, everyone trying to hold back the determined Germans.

They succeeded. By the end of December, Patton's tanks rolled even farther into Belgium. On the other side of the fight, German Panzers started to run out of fuel. Stalled and stuck, the Panzers turned into easy targets for the Allied tanks and fighter bombers. With the weather continuing to cooperate, Allied air forces flew as many as 500 sorties (or missions) a day.

The German army fell into full retreat.

By January 28th, the Battle of the Bulge was over. Forty-three days, 600,000 Allied troops, thousands of tanks and planes, and more than 100,000 casualties among the American forces alone—but the Allies had won.

Sadly, another 50,000 American soldiers were captured by the Germans. Another 23,000 were either missing or captured.

Germany casualties equaled the Allies. But Germany was too weak to replace its lost men and armaments. Worse for Hitler, he'd just lost his chance to force the Allies into peace negotiations.

For Adolf Hitler, the Battle of the Bulge would mark the beginning of the end.

WHO FOUGHT?

The German military feared only one Allied leader—General George S. Patton. They called Patton "The Cowboy General" because of his habit of carrying ivory-handed revolvers and wearing cavalry-style jodhpurs and riding boots.

During WWI, when Patton was a senior tank officer, he mastered blistering maneuvers for mechanized vehicles. By WWII, Patton was combining those maneuvers with sly strategies and tactics—and unbridled aggression. During the invasions of North Africa and Sicily, Patton's passionate style inspired every emotion among his men, from loyalty to hate. His superiors were just as divided. Patton's other nickname was "Old Blood and Guts."

Yet everyone agreed that Patton was a powerful leader. Despite taking on more enemy troops than other units, Patton's forces achieved quicker victories with fewer casualties.

In 1944, after his success in North Africa, Patton was temporarily relieved of command after he slapped a wounded soldier and accused another of faking his injury. Patton called these wounded soldiers cowards. The military disciplined him by forbidding his participation in the invasion of Sicily.

However, when it came time to beat Hitler in Belgium, Eisenhower called Patton.

The Cowboy General said many memorable things. Here are just three:

- "May God have mercy on my enemies, because I won't."
- "I don't measure a man's success by how high he climbs but by how high he bounces when he hits bottom."
- "The real hero is the man who fights even though he's scared."

Patton survived some of the deadliest and bloodiest battles known to man. In 1945, he died in a car accident in France. That same year, on Christmas Day, Patton was buried in a Belgian cemetery that was dedicated to the Americans who perished in the Battle of the Bulge.

In that cemetery, the Cowboy General joined six thousand of his men from the Third Army.

BOOKS

Soldier Boys by Dean Hughes

United States Army in WWII The Ardennes: Battle of the Bulge by Dr. Hugh M. Cole

Panther vs. Sherman: Battle of the Bulge 1944 (Duel) by Steven Zaloga, Jim Laurier, and Howard Gerrard

The Dead of Winter: How Battlefield Investigators, WWII Veterans, and Forensic Scientists Solved the Mystery of the Bulge's Lost Soldiers by Bill Warnock

The Battle of the Bulge by Veterans of the Battle of the Bulge

George S. Patton: World War II General & Military Innovator by Martin Gitlin

General George Patton: Old Blood & Guts by Alden Hatch

INTERNET

Short video with footage from the battlefield of Belgium: history.com/topics/world-war-ii/battle-of-the-bulge

Quick biography of General Patton: history.com/topics/world-war-ii/battle-of-the-bulge/videos/george-s-patton

The Library of Congress offers an interactive essay that shows how the "bulge" was created over the course of the battle, day by day: memory.loc.gov/ammem/collections/maps/wwii/essay1.html

MOVIES

Battle of the Bulge Patton

American Experience (PBS): The Battle of the Bulge

THE HOLOCAUST

Nazi soldiers gathering Jewish people. Notice the Star of David on the man's coat.

IN 1933, THE Nazis decided to convert a gun powder factory in Dachau, Germany into a prison.

Hitler needed the prison to lock up all the people who disagreed with his National Socialist—or "Nazi"—government.

Its first year, Dachau prison held 4,800 people. Soon, more structures were added to the prison, each one built by the Dachau prisoners forced into slave labor. A sign hanging over Dachau's entrance read: "Work makes one free." Of course, that was a lie. On November 11, 1938, waves of riots swept through Germany, Austria, and Czechoslovakia.

Nazi followers smashed the windows of Jewish homes, stores, and businesses.

That night was known as *Kristallnacht* or Night of the Breaking Glass.

About 30,000 Jews were rounded up on *Kristallnacht* and sent to prison camps like Dachau. Jews who didn't get sent to camps were forced to live in ghettos. They had to wear a large Star of David emblem on their clothing, identifying them as Jewish.

Hitler believed in a master race called Aryans. These people had blue eyes, white skin, and fair hair. Hitler and his Nazi followers were "cleansing" Germany of every race other than Aryan. They also wanted to kill anyone who they considered weak, such as the handicapped.

After invading European countries such as Poland, Hitler's cleansing philosophy spread to those conquered countries, and Dachau became the model for many more prison camps. These new camps sometimes had gas chambers and large ovens. They were called "extermination camps."

Nazi soldiers and police tormenting a Jewish man in Poland during WWII

One of Hitler's first actions as Germany's leader was to confiscate all privately owned firearms. That meant the people inside the Jewish ghettos didn't have any guns to defend themselves. To protect their families, men inside the ghettos developed clever street fighting techniques.

As the persecution continued, and more and more Jews disappeared into prison camps, pockets of Jewish resistance rose up. In Warsaw, Poland, ghetto dwellers attacked Nazi tanks with Molotov cocktails, hand grenades, and a tiny collection of illegal firearms. The uprising lasted several days.

But the fully-armed German soldiers and military police caught, killed, or shipped out every person inside the ghetto. Some of the Jewish resisters managed to hide inside the ghetto's ruins or escape into the forest. They lived in secret, scavenging for food, for the rest of the war.

Jews in Warsaw, Poland, captured after the ghetto uprising. They would be sent to concentration camps.

In the prison camps, inmates were tattooed with numbers on their wrist and held in spare wooden barracks guarded by armed guards. Some of the guards lived at the camps, too, but a courtyard separated them from the prisoners. The courtyard was often used to publicly torture or execute prisoners—to scare the other prisoners into obeying. Electrified barbed wire surrounded the prison camps and guard towers overlooked every area. If a prisoner tried to escape, the guards shot them.

Inmates were forced to work in camp laundries, kitchens, and bathrooms. Others served as household help for the Nazi officers and their families.

As the Nazis sent in Jews from France, Italy, Norway, and Denmark, the camps grew crowded. Gas chambers and crematoriums were added to "exterminate" whole populations of prisoners. Guards would round up prisoners, telling them it was time for a shower, and strip them naked. The locked shower room would then fill with poisonous gas, slowly killing everyone inside. Dead bodies were burned in the crematoriums—but only after the Nazis had removed anything valuable, such as gold fillings in teeth.

At Dachau alone, an estimated 100,000 prisoners died. Many of them starved to death.

These prison camps were sometimes located near German villages. People living near the camps heard rumors about what the Nazis were doing to these inmates. They also couldn't help but notice the greasy smoke that rose from the camp's chimneys. But these people chose to deny the rumors, or they agreed with the Nazi propaganda. Hitler's party was very effective at using euphemistic phrases—words that sound nicer than what's actually happening—to explain their murderous mission. For instance, one Nazi euphemism for mass murdering Jews was "The Final Solution to the Jewish Question." Another euphemism for killing handicapped or mentally ill people was "Life unworthy of life."

History is full of tribal wars. One particular group hates another group and wants them dead. But in terms of numbers, nothing compares to the Nazi Holocaust. In less than ten years, the Nazis killed more than *six million* Jews as well as another *five million* "inferior" people.

How did the Nazis manage this terrible feat? They built a highly sophisticated network of Jewish ghettos, railroads that led to concentration camps, and efficient crematoriums. They did it all while fighting the Allies.

"Consider why Germany, fighting a war on two fronts, desperate for fuel and materiel of every sort, would bother to load millions of Jews on railroad cars and transport them hundreds, even thousands, of miles to concentration camps," wrote author Edgar J. Steele. "Camps built specifically to house them, where they would be fed, clothed, even tattooed so they could be inventoried... just to kill them."

It sounds crazy, but hate motivated Hitler and his henchmen. Hatred of Jews spread across Europe.

By 1945, Germany and its allies were maintaining more than 42,000 concentration camps, prisons, and Jewish ghettos. This map shows only the major camps, while thousands more existed throughout Europe.

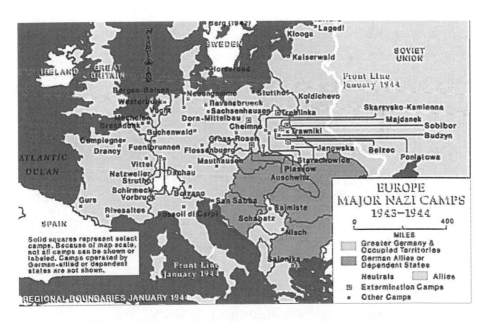

Map courtesy United States Holocaust Memorial Museum

German physicians also experimented on prison inmates. The doctors used them as lab rats to create new methods for building Hitler's "master race."

The most famous of these Nazi physicians was Dr. Josef Mengele. He worked inside a concentration camp in Auschwitz, Germany. Mengele's many painful experiments included injecting chemicals into children's eyes. Mengele wanted to change their eye color from brown to blue—Nazis wanted only blue eyes. He also infected prisoners with diseases such as tuberculosis and malaria, supposedly to find new remedies. But Mengele often killed the "patient" in the process. Other times he froze prisoners alive to study the effects of hypothermia.

Like all the Nazis, Mengele kept highly detailed records of these experiments.

Vera Alexander was a Jewish inmate at Auschwitz. Her prison job was to care for fifty sets of Gypsy twins. Mengele was obsessed with twins because he believed their genetic information would help him increase the number of Aryans in the world.

"I remember one set of twins in particular," Alexander later recalled. "Guido and Ina, aged about four. One day, Mengele took them away. When they returned, they were in a terrible state: they had been sewn together, back-to-back, like Siamese twins. Their wounds were infected and oozing pus. They screamed day and night. Then their parents—I remember the mother's name was Stella—managed to get some morphine and they killed the children in order to end their suffering."

Some prisoners tried to fight back.

At the camp called Treblinka, they stole weapons and attacked the guards. At Auschwitz-Birkenau, more than 250 prisoners died during an uprising. Another 200 were executed for participating. Five women—four of them Jewish—helped supply the prisoners with explosives to blow up the crematorium. They were executed, too.

Dead bodies placed in rows cover the prison yard of the Boelcke-Kaserne, a German concentration camp

After the decisive Allied win at the Battle of the Bulge, American armies began moving into Germany. In April, 1945, the US Army's 45th and 42nd divisions were ordered to travel to Dachau.

Realizing the Allies were coming, Dachau's camp guards quickly tried to hide evidence of Nazi brutality. Most people outside Germany had no idea about these camps, or what was happening inside them.

On April 29, American soldiers were following railroad

tracks through the town of Dachau when they saw a line of boxcars sitting on the rails. Guns raised, ready for a German attack, the Americans approached. A rotten stench filled the air. When the soldiers opened the boxcars, they found human corpses—more than 2,000 men, women, and children. "Tears were in everyone's eyes from the sight and smell," said Private 1st Class John Lee, who was among those soldiers.

Suddenly, four Nazi guards appeared, hands raised in surrender.

Lieutenant William P. Walsh led the four Germans into one of the railcars and emptied his pistol into their bodies. Walsh's action created a controversy that continues to this day. More than 500 Nazi prison guards were later prosecuted or executed for war crimes. But no Americans were prosecuted, including Lieutenant Walsh.

American soldiers liberating Dachau prison camp in April, 1945

Inside Dachau, prisoners heard the gunfire. When they saw the American soldiers, they realized what was happening. The soldiers broke through gates. Prisoners grabbed them, kissed them, even lifted them to their shoulders with sudden strength. However, other prisoners turned on the inmates who had cooperated with the Nazis or worked as informants for the guards. With their bare hands, prisoners killed the traitors.

Later that night, the American soldiers struggled to sleep, haunted by the horrors they'd seen at the camps.

General Eisenhower made it a priority to visit one of these German prison camps.

"I visited every nook and cranny of the camp," Eisenhower explained, "because I felt it my duty to be in a position from then on to testify firsthand about these things in case there ever grew up at home the belief or assumption that 'the stories of the Nazi brutality were just propaganda.'"

Eisenhower ordered his troops to document everything inside the camps. He sent dispatches to Washington, D.C. and London, calling for journalists and photographers. Eisenhower knew that ordinary people wouldn't believe these events unless they saw proof for themselves.

He also ordered his troops to gather up the German citizens who lived near these camps.

"We made the civilians who lived around there [Dachau] parade past the boxcars full of dead bodies," recalled Medic Peter Galary. "They said, 'We never knew about it.' They cried, but what good is crying going to do? It wouldn't bring any of those people back to life."

In total, the Holocaust killed about eleven million people, including one million children.

Just as Eisenhower predicted, today you can find people

who say the Holocaust never happened. Known as "Holocaust deniers," these people insist the Nazi slaughter of eleven million people was just a fable, a made-up story.

Facts, however, say otherwise.

WHO FOUGHT?

When Emrich "Imi" Lichtenfeld was twenty-six years old, Germany adopted the "Nuremburg Laws." These rules stated that Jews were inferior citizens who didn't deserve the same protection under the law as non-Jewish German citizens.

Imi Lichtenfeld had grown up wrestling, boxing, and weight lifting. When the German police took away all their weapons and started attacking him and his friends for being Jewish, Lichtenfeld realized his people needed new ways to protect themselves.

He gathered a bunch of Jewish boxers and wrestlers. These men patrolled the streets, defending Jewish neighborhoods from the Nazis and other Germans who hated Jews.

But Lichtenfeld soon realized that the kind of boxing and wrestling he did in competitions wouldn't work on the streets.

Examining his skills and techniques, he devised new ways to neutralize an enemy within seconds, especially when the only weapon was his bare hands. Litchenfeld's principles grew into a system of simultaneous defense and attack.

In 1940, realizing what was happening to Jews in Germany, Lichtenfeld escaped Europe on the last refugee ship. After a series of death-defying adventures, he landed in Israel. After the war, the United Nations granted Israel statehood, and Lichtenfeld started working with the brand-new Israeli Defense Force. He taught the soldiers his methods for ghetto street fighting. Those methods were the foundation of a martial arts known as Krav Maga.

Krav Maga is considered among the most powerful hand-to-hand combat styles in the world. It's still used by Israeli Defense forces.

Read more about Krav Maga here:

youtube.com/watch?v=J06kUz6v56I

BOOKS

Hitler Youth: Growing Up in Hitler's Shadow by Susan Campbell Bartoletti

The Nazi Hunters: How a Team of Spies and Survivors Captured the World's Most Notorious Nazi by Neal Bascomb

The Hidden Children of the Holocaust: Teens Who Hid from the Nazis by Esther Kustanowitz

The Hiding Place by Corrie Ten Boom

His Name Was Raoul Wallenberg by Louise W. Borden

How Huge the Night by Heather Munn

Surviving the Angel of Death: The True Story of a Mengele Twin in Auschwitz by Eva Mozes Kor and Lisa Rojany Buccieri

The Liberator: One World War II Soldier's 500-Day Odyssey from the Beaches of Sicily to the Gates of Dachau by Alex Kershaw

INTERNET

The United States Holocaust Memorial Museum is the best place to start an online journey into learning more about the Holocaust. Photos, videos, and survivor's stories—you'll find it all here: www.ushmm.org

This short film has rare historical footage showing the early persecution of Jews in Germany, which eventually led to the Holocaust: www.ushmm.org/learn/introduction-to-the-holocaust/path-to-nazi-genocide

Historic photos of Dachau prison camp: fcit.usf.edu/HOLOCAUST/RESOURCE/GALLERY/DACHAU.htm

"What Anne Frank's Arrest Looked Like" shows her final day of semi-freedom, before being captured by the Nazis: mentalfloss.com/article/58121/what-anne-franks-arrest-looked

MOVIES

Auschwitz—Inside the Nazi State

The Boy in the Striped Pajamas

Schindler's List

Shoah

Resistance: Untold Stories of Jewish Partisans

Diary of Anne Frank

Life is Beautiful

Hidden in Silence

VICTORY IN EUROPE: V-E DAY

May 8, 1945

American Military Police on a road inside Germany, May, 1945

THE EVENTS THAT led to the end of WWII went like this:

January, 1945: The Allies won the Battle of the Bulge. Stalin's Red Army breached the Eastern Front, and the Soviets began marching toward Berlin, the capital of Germany.

February: The Allies also moved toward Germany from the west.

March: Hitler continued to lose battles, men, and armaments. Casualties among German forces numbered in the millions. Germany didn't have enough fuel and arms to continue fighting, but Hitler was a madman and refused to surrender.

April: United States President Franklin Roosevelt died in office. His Vice President, Harry Truman, was named in his place.

Hitler took the news about Roosevelt's death as a hopeful sign, believing the Allies would fall apart and Germany would win the war. Against advice of his military leaders, Hitler stayed in Berlin, living in a bunker under the city. Mentally, Hitler had snapped. One moment he would fly into rages and insist Germany must win this war; the next moment he would scream that they all deserved to die.

Hitler's bunker after Berlin was captured

April 20: The Battle of Berlin. Stalin's forces arrived from the east with nearly 2.5 million men to fight Germany, which had only 700,000 men, all of them exhausted and starving.

Stalin also had 7,500 planes. The Luftwaffe had only 2,000.

In every category that mattered, the lopsided numbers told the same story.

General Eisenhower chose not to rush into Berlin right away. The Allies had suffered enough casualties. Eisenhower believed the city would fall to the Soviets. However, the Allies did help Stalin by bombing Berlin for thirty-six nights in a row.

April 25: Soviet and Allied forces met at the Elbe River in Germany.

April 30: Deep inside his bunker, Hitler wrote his political testament and named his successor, Admiral Karl Dönitz. Hitler then swallowed cyanide poison which killed him. Many of his officers also committed suicide. Some even gave the deadly poison to their children.

May 2: The Battle of Berlin ended. The Soviets crushed the Germans, who, just six years earlier, had conquered Poland, Norway, France, Czechoslovakia, Belgium, Romania, and Bulgaria. Hitler's Third Reich was reduced to a heap of dust and ruins.

Berlin, 1945

May 5: Nazi leaders realized surrender was their only option. But Admiral Dönitz and other German leaders feared the Soviets. German soldiers had committed many atrocities against the Russians during the war. Dönitz wanted to negotiate an exclusive surrender to the Allies—cutting out the Soviets. But his efforts failed. In a schoolhouse in Reims, France, negotiations for surrender began. German General Alfred Jodl requested a 48-hour delay of the surrender, because German soldiers were still fighting on the Eastern Front. Jodl wanted these men to be able to withdraw before the Soviets killed them.

Eisenhower refused the request. As Supreme Leader of the Allied Forces, Eisenhower had watched Germans slaughter his troops. He had just witnessed the gruesome Nazi prison camps. Eisenhower felt little mercy for the Germans. But Jodl tried again, insisting a delay would help the Allies, too, because the

Soviets would become enemies of America and continue spreading their Communist political system around the world.

"You'll be fighting the Russians yourself," Jodl told Eisenhower. "Save as many Germans as you can for them."

Eisenhower agreed that Soviet Communism was a problem, but he still refused Jodl's request for extra time to surrender.

Finally, Jodl sent a message to the new German government. There was "no alternative other than sign, or chaos."

May 7: At 2:35 a.m., German delegates sat down at a table inside the French schoolhouse. At 2:41 a.m., Jodl signed the Act of Military Surrender.

The text reads in part: "We, the undersigned, acting by authority of the German High Command, hereby surrender unconditionally to the Supreme Commander, Allied Expeditionary Forces, and simultaneously to the Soviet High Command, all forces on land, sea, and in air who are at this date under German control."

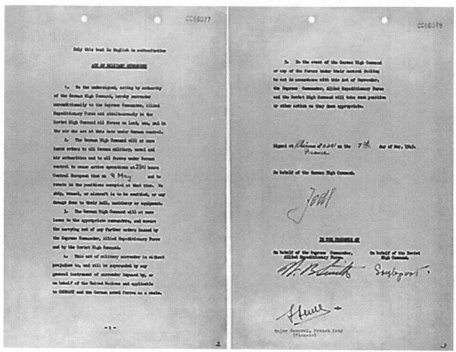

German Instrument of Surrender, signed. It didn't require many words, did it?

Hoping to escape capture by the Soviets, about one million German soldiers tried to flee to safety.

But Stalin's men caught many of them. The Soviets kept two million Germans as prisoners of war.

For the Allies, however, the surrender brought release. More than 95,000 American POWs were set free, along with 13,000 British soldiers.

May 8: With news of the surrender, mass celebrations broke out in England. Floodlights gleamed from Buckingham Palace—the first time in six years, since London first instituted blackouts at the start of the war. And above St. Paul's Cathedral, two searchlights intersected to form a giant "V" for Victory.

Winston Churchill lifts the sign of "V" for Victory above the gathered crowd in
London, May 8, 1945

In the United States, the celebrations stretched from coast to coast. Church bells rang. Train conductors blew their horns. Cab drivers honked. People literally danced in the streets.

However, the celebrations were short-lived. American soldiers were still fighting the Japanese. The day after Germany surrendered, a Japanese kamikaze pilot flew his plane into an Allied aircraft carrier—a grim reminder of the fight still ahead.

To win World War II, the Allies still needed to defeat Japan. The question was—could they?

If you'd like to read about the thrilling battles in WWII's Pacific campaign, click here for *Great Battles for Boys: WWII The Pacific.*

END NOTE

I hope you enjoyed reading about some of WWII's European battles. But I also hope this book is just the beginning of your journey into history. Even after decades of reading and studying military battles, I'm still learning more about them. Below are some of the books that helped me put together these battles for you.

An Army At Dawn: The War in North Africa by Rick Atkinson

The Day of Battle: The War in Sicily and Italy, 1943–1944 by Rick Atkinson

D-Day by Stephen Ambrose

Citizen Soldiers by Stephen Ambrose

Comrades by Stephen Ambrose

Allies: Pearl Harbor to D-Day by John S.D. Eisenhower

Stalingrad by Anthony Beevor

Lost Victories by Erich von Manstein

Rifles of the White Death by Doug Bowser

Ghost Soldiers by Hampton Sides

Writers on World War II edited by Mordecai Richler

George C. Marshall by Mark A. Stoler

The Guns of August by Barbara Tuchman

War As I Knew It by George S. Patton, Paul D. Harkins and Rick Atkinson

Magazines

MHQ: The Quarterly Journal of Military History. Volume 11, 1998
    World War II magazine: *50th Anniversary of the D-Day Invasion*

Battle of Kursk: Germany's Lost Victory in World War II by George M.
    Nipe, Jr.

Avalanche: How Both Sides Lost at Salerno by Robert M. Citino

Some Websites

With nearly 20,000 photographs from WWII, including daily
updates on historic battles, the World War II Database provides
invaluable resources:
ww2db.com/index.php

The website for the 505th Parachute Infantry Regiment during
WWII has plenty of information on paratroopers:
www.ww2-airborne.us/units/505/505.html

United States Holocaust Memorial Museum is among the very
best places to learn more about this tragic history:
www.ushmm.org

Awesome Stories has many good explanations of battles,
especially "Stalingrad: Deadly Battle of WWII" by Carole Bos:
www.awesomestories.com/asset/view/Stalingrad-Deadly-
Battle-of-WWII

For information about Stalin and his forces, information can be
found at Russia Beyond the Headlines, including for the Battle
of Kursk:
rbth.com/society/2013/07/12/eyewitness_accounts_of_the_ba
ttle_of_kursk_28009.html

ABOUT THE AUTHOR

JOE GIORELLO grew up in a large Italian family in Queens, New York, hearing firsthand stories from relatives who served in World War II and Vietnam. Those stories sparked his love of history and spurred him into studying military history. He's since acquired a vast library, stretching from ancient battles to modern warfare, and teaches a highly popular middle-grade class called "Great Battles." As both a teacher and an author, Joe's goal is to remind young people that "freedom isn't free" and that history is anything but boring. When he's not teaching about historic battles, weapons, and warfare, Joe can be found playing blues around the Seattle area with his band, The Fabulous Roof Shakers.

Joe really likes hearing from readers. Contact him at his website: www.greatbattlesforboys.com. Be sure to sign up for Joe's newsletter so you can be among the first to hear about new battle books in this series.

You can also contact Joe on Facebook at facebook.com/greatbattles

Made in the USA
Middletown, DE
06 May 2020